Jean Marc

Regards,

P.W.

a measure
of Value

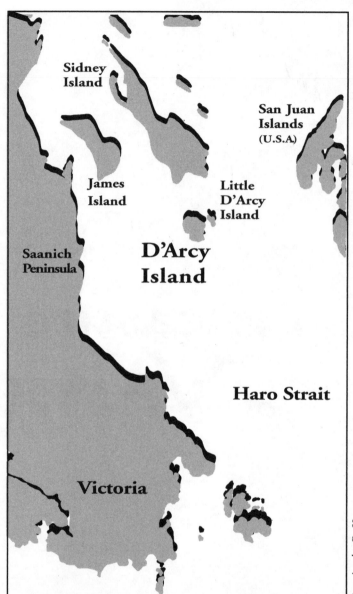

Drawing by R. Kung

C. J. YORATH

a measure of Value

the Story of the D'Arcy Island Leper Colony

TouchWood Editions

CANADIAN CATALOGUING IN PUBLICATION DATA

Yorath, C. J., 1936-
    A measure of value

Includes bibliographical references and index.
ISBN 0-920663-73-7

1. Leprosy—British Columbia—D'Arcy Island—History. I. Title.

RC154.55.C32D378 2000   362.1'96998'00971128
C00-910841-6

First edition 2000

Horsdal & Schubart acknowledge the financial support of the Government of Canada through the Canada Council for the Arts and the Book Publishing Industry Development Program (BPIDP) for our publishing activities. We also acknowledge the assistance of the Province of British Columbia, through the British Columbia Arts Council.

Cover and text design by Catherine Hart
Photos and maps by author, unless otherwise noted in photo credits on page 174.

TOUCHWOOD EDITIONS
An imprint of Horsdal & Schubart Publishers Ltd.
Victoria/Surrey, BC, Canada
touchwoodeditions@home.com

Printed and bound in Canada
Canadä

Contents

Courage: A man stands alone in a field filled with grass, facing wild creatures and enduring nature's hardships.

 Destiny: The law of nature and the destiny of life is death.

 Eternity: The sun always rises, the moon pulls the tides, the water continues to flow.

 Honor: In Taoism, honor is an inner quality more precious than jade, yet frequently hidden under humble clothing.

 Melancholy: A bittersweet feeling that comes when contemplating the cycle of life and death, fullness and decay.

THIS BOOK IS DEDICATED TO THE MEN
WHO LIVED AND DIED ON D'ARCY ISLAND, BRITISH COLUMBIA,
BETWEEN THE YEARS 1891 AND 1906.

Sim Lee

Ng Chung

Chin You

Nap Sing

Ah Chee

Oung Moi Toy

Alexander Sundy

? Sing

Ah Lung

Chin Wah Yuen

Lang Nung

Lim Sam

Ah Sing

Lung Hing

and perhaps others,
names unknown

Foreword

BETWEEN 1891 AND 1924, 49 people were exiled to D'Arcy Island to suffer the debilitating effects of leprosy in isolation. The great majority were Chinese.

The inhospitable environment characterizing this "island prison" is a poignant analogy for the racial bias and discrimination that led to the decision to banish those afflicted with this disease—a decision utterly devoid of compassion.

Indeed, when waves of Chinese immigrants began arriving on Canada's shores in the late 1800s to help build the Canadian Pacific Railway their new home was far removed from the "Golden Mountain" they had envisioned. They worked in jobs that were dangerous—jobs that nobody else wanted—for minimal pay. It has been estimated that six Chinese lives were lost for every mile of track laid.

The terror they faced at work was no doubt matched by the fear and social alienation they confronted "off the job." Discrimination against Chinese immigrants manifested itself in many ways, including the imposition of a head tax, the enactment of discriminatory immigration laws and the withholding of voting rights. It is sadly ironic that the very freedoms enjoyed by Canadians today were not afforded to those whose descendants fought for Canada in two world wars.

Having recently been elected the fiftieth Mayor of the City of Victoria, and the first of Chinese ancestry, I now represent the very organization that ordered the detainment and imprisonment of those sent to D'Arcy Island a century ago. My election symbolizes the progress we as a society have made in protecting, and embracing, the differences that distinguish Canada as a cultural, racial and religious mosaic.

As Canadians we have much to be proud of—our social programs and standard of living are the envy of the world. Our identity as Canadians is inextricably linked with our commitment to social justice. Our pride should not, however, blind us to the realities, and lessons, of our past mistakes. In forgetting the past we risk repeating it, as was eloquently said by George Santayana.

I am extremely proud to be a Chinese Canadian and am committed to promoting the values of respect, compassion and tolerance in an effort to ensure that future Canadians find Victoria a hospitable and welcoming "home"—in honour of the "crying souls" of D'Arcy Island.

Alan Lowe, Mayor, City of Victoria
May 30, 2000

Acknowledgments

I AM INDEBTED to Dr. Paul Brand for his critical review of the chapter on leprosy and for providing many valuable suggestions for its improvement. I express gratitude to the archivists of the British Columbia Archives, and those of the City of Victoria Archives, Trevor Livelton and Carey Pallister, all of whom deserve much credit for their patient guidance of my research. Clifford Cornish, manager of Library Services for the Capital Health Region as well as library staff of the Greater Victoria Public Library and the McPherson Library of the University of Victoria gave valuable assistance as did Chris Kissinger, Sherrie Gardner and Robert Austad of the Southern Gulf Islands District of B.C. Parks. I thank Dr. Kelin Wang and Robert Kung for helping me to understand Chinese culture and Marilyn Bowering, author of *To All Appearances A Lady*, for helpful conversations.

I express my thanks to Sheldon and Mark Green for boat trips to D'Arcy Island and especially the former for his assistance in the discovery of the original site of the lazaretto. I thank Norman Jonasson for his help in identifying critical characteristics of the original building site. I am indebted to Erik Paulsson who provided much useful information arising from his research for a television documentary on the history of the D'Arcy Island leper colony, a project in which he invited me to participate.

Several other people provided valuable help; these include Dan Dobson and Rikki Farrel of the Canadian Hydrographic Service at the Institute of Ocean Sciences, Lynn Wright of the Maritime Museum of British Columbia, staff of the Provincial Surveyor General's Office and Dr. Gilbert Chew, my family's physician, who gave guidance in regard to leprosy research and resources among the Chinese community of Victoria. Kyle Hyndman gave helpful comments regarding the legal aspects of the lazaretto's establishment. I am most grateful to my wife Linda for her endless patience and thorough editing of early versions of the manuscript as well as to my friend Donald Cook who read parts of the manuscript for interest and readability. Finally, and most importantly, I thank Heather Carter-Simmons for her exhaustive search for contemporary newspaper articles on the D'Arcy Island leper colony.

Introduction

THIS BOOK IS about 23 men, mostly Chinese, who, between the years 1891 and 1906, were stockpiled to die on a tiny island not far from Victoria, British Columbia. What was common among them was leprosy, a disease that elicited feelings of horror and dread no different in the nineteenth and twentieth centuries from those felt by the people of Europe during the Dark and Middle Ages. It is a tale of fear and medical ignorance, of irresponsibility and political arrogance. Against an undercurrent of sometimes egregious anti-Chinese racial prejudice, the residents of D'Arcy Island lived in a monotony of timeless suffering until death claimed their emaciated bodies. No records. No memories.

As the second of Canada's two lazarettos,[1] the D'Arcy Island facility was established by the Victoria municipal government to confine, house, feed and clothe five leprous men found living in the city's Chinatown. As news of the lazaretto spread, other communities throughout the province also passed responsibility for their "unfortunates" on to the city which, over a period of 15 years, tried to persuade the dominion government to assume responsibility for their care as it had done at Tracadie, New Brunswick. Following passage of the Leprosy Act in 1906 the dominion government managed the facility until 1924, after which leprosy patients were confined to Bentinck Island near the William Head Quarantine Station west of Victoria.

The Prologue and its continuations throughout the text are a fictional account of one man's journey from China to Victoria, Nanaimo and finally D'Arcy Island. It is intended to give the reader some idea of who these people were and how it was that they had their lives taken from them by disease and fear. It is my attempt to give them humanity. Chapter One is a discussion of the disease of leprosy, or, more properly, Hansen's disease. Here I describe its history, epidemiology, pathology and treatment. I also discuss its extraordinary stigma, which has persisted and remained unchanged since pre-biblical times. Whereas the characterizations and public perceptions of other diseases, equally metaphorical, have changed through time, those of leprosy seem to be immutable. Chapters Two, Three and Four together provide a detailed account of what is known of the history of the lazaretto, concentrating upon its first fifteen years. Chapter Five is a commentary on that history; although much is known of what the *authorities* did in respect of the facility, little is known of just how the residents managed on a day-to-day basis and how they organized themselves into a society which survived as a constantly changing micro-civilization in spite of extraordinary difficulties.

In writing this book I have attempted to take the middle road between apologism and anger. Because of the often extreme anti-Chinese racial prejudice expressed by the press and politicians at the time the lazaretto was established, it would have been very easy for me to cast blame upon them and to express every nuance of the lazaretto's history in racist terms. Indeed, at least one student of the subject has done so. It would be easy for someone to see ugliness and hatred in all that the "whites" did. On the other hand it must be acknowledged that, at that time of economic depression and racial prejudice, the Chinese lepers had little chance of employment or assistance, even from their own countrymen. At the very least, the Corporation of the City of Victoria gave them the means to survive until the disease, or its consequences, consumed them. I am not an apologist for the medical health officers' lack of proper practice nor for the City of Victoria's nearly panicked reaction to the discovery of lepers in its midst. Rather, I have attempted to tell the history as revealed in documents and to comment upon several aspects of that history, without prejudice.

Throughout this book I use the word "leper" commonly. It is an ugly word, indivisibly attached to myth and immutable stigma. I use the words "residents" and "men," but not "patients" because, until 1906, they were nobody's patients. Phrases such as "sufferers of Hansen's disease" are awkward. Not being an advocate of historical revisionism, currently popular, I am reluctant to alter the mood that words convey and thereby tinker with the cultural and intellectual environments within which they were used. Leper is an ugly word. So is this story.

The book is based mainly upon documents from the City of Victoria Archives, British Columbia Archives and the National Archives of Canada and over 190 contemporary newspaper articles in the Victoria *Daily Colonist* and *Daily Times,* as well as the Vancouver *Province, Daily News Advertiser* and *Daily World.* A list and copies of the press articles, as well as reproductions of other documents, are held by the City of Victoria Archives. Numerous other sources including books, journal articles, research theses and Internet web-pages are listed in the bibliography. People and place names introduced in the Prologue are real. Based on the limited information available I have recreated the events described, and the details contained on the official immigration form.

Prologue

ABOVE THE WIND IT DRIFTS,
REACHING FOR EMPTY SPACE,
THERE TO SOAR ON RIGID WHITE WINGS.

IT GAZES DOWN ON ME, ITS ORANGE BEAK SPOT
POINTING THIS WAY THEN THAT. A CALLING SCREECH
BEFORE IT LANDS. ALONE. TO DIE ON A BEACH
AT THE PLACE WITH NO NAME.

ANOTHER DRIFTS UPWARD TO TAKE ITS PLACE.

DURING THE TIME he had been sitting on the log the tide had changed twice. Sacks of rice. Barrels of salt pork. Two coffins. A crate full of chickens. Some blankets, a mirror and pairs of overshoes. And opium, for a treat. It was June 15, 1899. Dr. Fraser and some others had come. Captain Clark and the crew of the *Sadie* had carried the supplies onto the beach, but not until he and the others were on the veranda up at the house. Once they ran down to the beach to meet the men who dropped everything and ran away. The men said they wouldn't come again unless the lepers stayed on the veranda. He looked down at his overshoes.

Out in Haro Strait he could see boats pass by the island, most headed for the fishing grounds on the Fraser. They never stopped, or even slowed down, even when the flag was on the pole. For a while they put the flag on the pole when one of them was dying. Nobody came so they stopped doing it. He looked down at his overshoes again. He could see the stumps of what were once his toes through the hole in the end of the right one. There was blood. Always blood.

He knew that when he put his hand in the fire he could leave it there for a long time. Till his skin went black and blistery. The smell would tell him to take his hand out of the fire. He smiled to himself. Maybe I can go home if I'm all burnt.

The *Empress of China* was tied up at the wharf below the quarantine station at Albert Head, a few miles west of Victoria. About 450 men, mostly Chinese from near Canton, were lined up for inspection by medical authorities. When it was his turn he gave answers to an interpreter, who in turn translated for the man who filled in the form, in long horizontal rows:

Serial No: 28.651

Port No. of Statement of Declaration: 15511

Name: Lim Sam

Port or Place Where Registered: Victoria

Date of Registration: October 19, 1891

Certificate Issued:

    C.I.   5 No. 22682

    C.I. 6 No. 164193

Fees Paid: Amount: $50.00

Sex: Male

Age: 24

Place of Birth: China

City or Village: Chunwan

District: Sun Way

Title, Official Rank, Profession or Occupation:

    Gardener

Last Place of Domicile: Hong Kong

Arrival in Canada

Port or Place Of: Victoria

Name of Vessel, Railway or other Conveyance:

    Empress of China

Date Of: October 18, 1891

Physical Marks or Peculiarities:

    Small stature. Round face. Long pigtail.
    Prominent scar on upper right arm—caused by
    a knife when he was young. Slight limp or
    shuffle.

Remarks: No visible symptoms of communicable
or infectious disease.

Lim Sam was glad when it was over. At last he had reached North America. The Manchus and foreigners had made life for him and his family in China very difficult. There was little work and what he could get paid poorly. Besides, there always seemed to be a war going on. If it wasn't with the British or Americans over opium, it was with the Koreans or someone else over something else. By the time he left China the country was mostly run by foreigners, and another war was brewing with the Japanese. He had been born in the village of Chunwan where, fifteen years later, his mother died giving birth to his younger brother. During the period before her death, his parents were able to send him to school for a few years where he learned to read and write; however, working conditions ultimately became so poor that his father, a tailor by trade, was unable to continue to support his education. When Lim Sam was 20 his father was diagnosed with leprosy and taken to the Presbyterian Mission at Canton. That was the last time he saw him.

Lim Sam was on the short and light side of average build. Large, widely set dark eyes separated a broad forehead from prominent high cheeks and a narrow, somewhat aquiline nose. His mouth was small, and he liked to tuck his queue beneath his lower lip when nothing was on his mind. About the only noteworthy things about him physically were his hands. They were large and muscular-looking, more than would be expected from the rest of his appearance. He was of average intelligence and possessed an average knowledge of his world. He was neither pretentious nor apologetic, was moderately gregarious and enjoyed the company of his friends.

After his father was taken away, Lim Sam resolved to go to North America, as many Chinese men had done before him. By then he had been married for five years and had a four-year-old son. He had heard from those returning that Canada was a good place to earn money to support a wife and child. Jobs were plentiful, so he was told, and the money he earned could be sent home to his family. He couldn't afford to take them with him because that would require more money than he could earn in China in four years. Besides, his wife's mother was ill. Maybe when she died he could send the money to bring them to Canada. His wife's name was Ah Lan. She had been raised in the same village and had been contracted to him when she was four. Although he beat her on occasion he was really very fond of her and allowed her to scold him when he got drunk, which wasn't often. Sometimes, when they were alone, they would hold hands and talk of the dreams they had the night before. She was very tiny with laughing black eyes that got progressively sadder as life in China got more and more difficult. When her younger sister drowned, the laughter left her eyes forever.

When Lim Sam left to find work in Hong Kong, Ah Lan stayed behind with their son and her mother. As he walked away from the small, two-room house, he occasionally looked back and saw her wave in the doorway, even when he was a long way away and she was very, very small. Almost too small to make a memory. He had learned there were many grand homes owned by foreigners in Hong Kong where he hoped to find employment, perhaps as a gardener, in which he had some experience. Apart from the small amount he would send to his wife, he planned to save as much money as he could so as to buy passage to Canada aboard one of the steamships or sailing vessels that carried passengers, cargo and mail. He learned that the fare would be about $100 plus an additional $50 for the head tax. He figured it would take him two to three years to make the money. He had learned of labour brokers who would grant passage to men in return for their being indentured for many years but this sounded too much like slavery. He preferred to be his own man.

A friend had told him of a boat that would take him to Hong Kong for five shillings so he started walking, but then he got a ride in a wagon to Guanghai on the coast where he found the boat tied up to the only wharf in the town. The drunken crew returned about midnight to find Lim Sam sitting on his pack on the dock beside the boat.

"I was told I might be able to get a ride to Kowloon," he said.

"You got five shillings?"

"Yes."

"That all right?" asked the man, looking at his companions.

They nodded.

After getting some sleep on board they left at first light. The sea was smooth with a gentle easterly swell passing across the South China Sea as they moved slowly along the coast where fishermen were casting nets, or, in small boats, drifting offshore and using diving cormorants to catch their prey. As they travelled northeastward during the next two days, passing the Portuguese town of Macao, more and more junks appeared, some filled with produce, others with people. Lim Sam had never seen such apparent chaos. There were junks and other boats of all shapes and sizes swarming about while sailing ships, sails tightly furled on their spars, rested majestically alongside the many wharves of Kowloon and Victoria. They passed inward- and outward-bound steamships, as well as awkward-looking tugs and barges, and at last found a berth at a crowded wharf near the eastern limits of Victoria. Lim Sam decided to get off here rather than at Kowloon, so after paying the helmsman he picked up his bundle and stepped ashore.

Above the harbour the hilly terrain of Hong Kong Island was taking on the appearance of the south of England. Since being ceded to the British at the Treaty of Nanking in 1842, ending the First Opium War, the island had attracted considerable numbers of wealthy British bureaucrats and military people who had constructed grand homes on the lower slopes above the town. Later, following the Treaty of Tientsin that ended the Second Opium War in 1858, the British also acquired Kowloon and nearby Stonecutters Island as well as greatly expanding their sphere of influence throughout southern China. It was among these interlopers—British civil servants, merchants and opportunists—that Lim Sam wanted to find work and also to learn English.

During the following two years Lim Sam was able to find occasional work as a gardener and general labourer. For most of that time he lived on an abandoned junk along with three other men; they had ambitions of going to the United States but the American Exclusion Act made that almost impossible. Upon learning this, Lim Sam was pleased that he had opted for Canada even though it imposed a $50 head tax on each new arrival. Toward the end of the two years he knew that it would take several more years before he had saved enough money to buy his passage. The labour-brokerage firm of Syme, Muir and Co., for the price of garnisheeing half of his wages for two years, offered to guarantee him a job in the Nanaimo coalfields operated by the Dunsmuir family and pay his passage to Canada. He soon realized that if he really wanted to go, he had no choice but to accept their offer, and on September 10 of 1891 he boarded the *Empress of China*. At 4:00 P.M. the lines were drawn and the gleaming white ship moved slowly out into Victoria Bay, sailed eastward past North Point, then turned south through Tathong Channel to thrust her bow into the South China Sea.

Some of the others were moving about on the beach, picking up what they could and carrying the supplies to the storage shed at the west end of the veranda. As Lim Sam sat gazing blankly down at his overshoes, he wondered when he was going to die. He turned his head to look out to sea. Along the distant shore he could see columns of smoke rising from piles of burning brush. He farted.

"Ah Sam,"[2] came a voice from nearby. "I've been looking for you. They brought the chess pieces. Want a game?" It was Chin Wah Yuen. He had been on the island for about four years and had managed to outlive many who had arrived before and after him.

Lim Sam looked up at him with weary, folded eyes. "Perhaps later," he mumbled. "I want to sit in the sun a while longer."

It was mid-afternoon and the sun was still high above the Malahat Range, to the west on Vancouver Island. Lim Sam's mind stumbled across disconnected memories. He had been on the island forever, without the means of knowing time or caring. He had been dying for many seasons, for many tides. For seven years. And he was tired. He was floating upon a vast ocean, waiting for the storm to sink him. The storm that would not come. The soupy, grey sea rolled gently beneath him, lifting and falling in an endless monotony of soundless symphony. Squalls would appear in the distance and sink someone else. But not him.

He had thought of death often, more in the past than now. Raised as a Buddhist he knew he would be reborn, either as another human being or as an animal, depending upon his behaviour and karma in this life. However, he hadn't considered that his karma included leprosy and that he would die on this tiny island, far removed from those Taoist values which, had he studied them, would have allowed him to return in a higher state of grace. Indeed, his leprosy was his suffering in this life, as it might well be in the next. Being a simple and unpretentious man, he had feared death as much as anybody when he was young but now, he was unafraid, because perhaps he was already dead. Perhaps the storm had come and gone, only to leave him floating lifeless upon the sea. With but one memory—a tiny woman waving to him from far, far away.

After passing through immigration, Lim Sam, along with many other immigrants, walked the 12 miles along the muddy road from the Albert Head Quarantine Station to Victoria. He walked among a small group of friends he had made on the Pacific crossing, all of whom, like him, were looking for work in order to support their families in China. It was a drizzly October day with low clouds hanging like grey aprons over the dark, brooding slopes of the Olympic Mountains on the far side of the Strait of Juan de Fuca. Only a few scattered homes heralded the growth of the satellite communities of Metchosin and Colwood; however, the town of Esquimalt was already well established around the naval base that clung to the rocky shores of its natural harbour. With directions provided by other immigrants who had arrived earlier, the procession at last found its way to Chinatown, which, at that time, was the largest Chinese community in Canada.

Developed mainly within the four-block area enclosed by Johnson, Fisgard, Douglas and Government streets, the community consisted of some 150 business firms, 2 theatres, 1 hospital, 3 schools, 2 churches and several temples and shrines. Behind the commercial facades a maze of narrow passageways and courtyards hid from public view many gambling dens, opium factories and brothels. Because he was told not to report for work in the Nanaimo coalfields until the following spring, it was into the Victoria Chinatown that Lim Sam temporarily vanished. He shared one-room accommodation with four others he had sailed with, running errands for a nearby grocer in return for food.

During the next few months Lim Sam found occasional work as a gardener at some of the larger homes along the Gorge and in the newly developing community of Oak Bay. The work was not steady, however, and with the arrival of winter, there was little at all. Most of what he had earned he needed to keep for himself and was unable to send any money home. In the early spring, with what little money he had saved, he bought a ticket on the Esquimalt and Nanaimo Railway and headed north.

As the train passed over the Malahat Range and descended into the Cowichan Valley, Lim Sam felt conspicuous and ill at ease. Since his arrival in Canada he had protectively confined himself mostly to an expatriate Chinese community, thereby not risking exposure among a strongly prejudiced white population. Now he was out there, travelling among them and again moving into an unfamiliar world. However, his fellow passengers took little notice of him or of the long queue extending down his back. He carried a broad-brimmed black hat and wore a brown shirt and black pants. His large, dark eyes rarely rested, darting nervously here and there with each unpredicted movement, both hands tightly grasping the cloth pack that held the few articles that defined him. At the Duncan station the train stopped to exchange some passengers, mostly local Indians.

After another stop at Ladysmith the train continued on to Nanaimo, a grimy little town composed of one-design company row-houses covered in coal dust. The commercial area boasted a couple of brick buildings but otherwise there was nothing to attract an itinerant visitor, or resident for that matter. Upon disembarking from the train Lim Sam wasted no time in finding the small Chinese community; there he was introduced to its power brokers who advised him how to behave in regard to working in the mines.

He was warned of strong, racist, union resistance to the hiring of cheap Chinese labour and that he should expect some hostility from white miners. They told him of the explosion in the Vancouver Coal Mining and Land Company's mine in May of 1887 that had killed 192 miners, including 75 Chinese. The white miners had blamed the disaster on the Chinese, which led to several strikes and unsuccessful petitions to the provincial legislature to prohibit Chinese from working in the mines. The Vancouver Coal Mining and Land Company succumbed to union pressure and excluded Chinese from their operations, but the mine operated by Dunsmuir and Sons Ltd. continued to employ them at one dollar a day while whites were paid twice that amount. Although publicly the militancy of the unions was strong, in reality it was tempered by their appreciation of the Chinese miners for doing the menial as well as the most dangerous work. The collieries mined coal from three seams underground and it was in these operations where Lim Sam was most likely to be put to work because it was there that the danger was greatest.

At the Dunsmuir mine office he presented the paper given to him by the labour broker in Hong Kong and the next day found himself sitting in a trolley being lowered into a shaft that extended well out beneath the bottom of Nanaimo harbour. The coal was enclosed within crumbly friable sandstone; thus, considerable quantities of timbers were used to support the shaft walls and roof. Nevertheless, because of the coal's highly volatile bituminous grade, gas explosions and rock breakouts were a constant threat to the miners, and they were content to have Chinese men around for the dirty stuff, such as the setting of fuses following emplacement of dynamite charges by the shooters.

As the weeks and months passed Lim Sam was able to send some of his earnings home, even though he saw only half of his wages. He even found that his acceptance among the white workers was enough to allow him to sit among them while they ate their lunches. Sometimes they would even kid him and once they asked about his home and what it was like to live in China. Sitting in the dark with only the light from his headlamp to illuminate his space, he saw his world as a closed blackness, occasionally punctuated by another lamp. Partly illuminated faces passed by, then blackness again. The black air and the black coal became a continuum in time and space, so much so that when he again reached the surface at the end of a shift, he was glad when it was night. It was on one of these shifts, deep underground and at the farthest end of the shaft, that he first noticed it. A small, hard, numb spot on the back of his left hand.

At first he tried to dismiss the discovery—probably it was due to a minor scrape, and what he was feeling was a scar. But even in the blackness of the shaft he soon knew that it wasn't a scar. In the light of his miner's lamp the patch seemed to be a hard, raised, dark lump, about the size of a quarter, with no feeling. He remembered his father and immediately felt his ear lobes—one seemed slightly swollen and harder than normal, but he might have been imagining this. He felt his lips but found no change. Fear began to spread through him. At the sound of the whistle signalling the end of his shift he moved quickly down the long shaft toward the trolley waiting to take him back to the surface. This was a daylight shift change and, although he was black with coal dust, he kept his face and hands hidden from view in case someone might notice.

Back in the small, one-room shack he and two friends rented for 50¢ a week, he quickly washed and began to examine himself for other evidence of the dreaded disease. Again he remembered his father's senseless hands, swollen lips and collapsed nose. By the time he had been taken away the disfigurement was ghastly, his face covered with draining tubercles and his fingers clenched like the claws of some mythical beast. In his father's case the disease had progressed so rapidly that from the time of its first symptoms until he was taken away was only about one year.

Lim Sam lay awake throughout that night, wondering what to do—how to avoid notice, and what would happen to him if he were discovered. He tried to convince himself that it was just as likely something else, but he knew it wasn't. Shortly before leaving Victoria he had heard of five Chinese lepers discovered living in a shack behind a store on Fisgard Street and that they had been deported to some nearby island. Apparently one of them had tried to slit his throat when he discovered what was going to happen to him; a policeman wrestled the knife away from him. Again he remembered his father and the horror crept through him. What could he do? Could he get back to China before anyone saw the effects of the disease? He would have to return to Victoria and get someone to buy a ticket for him, then somehow avoid the quarantine inspection and board the ship. Once on board he would probably be safe because, even if he were discovered, they would most likely be at sea, too far to turn back. If he left soon enough the leprosy would not have progressed sufficiently for anyone to notice, or so he hoped.

The more he thought about it the more determined he became to return home. For the next several weeks he continued to go to work. Saving every penny. Each day he concealed his face and hands as best he could until he was safe in the blackness underground. He avoided his shift-mates and ate his meals alone, away from them in a dark recess of the shaft. At the end of each shift he hurried home, hoping not to being seen. He stayed inside, away from the view of friends, or anyone who might see a change in his appearance. Day after day this routine went on while, gradually, red spots began to appear on his face and the back of his neck. He knew he had to make his move soon. Finally, the day came when he thought he had saved enough. This was to be his last shift. He would collect his last pay at the gate and tell them he wouldn't be back.

"Going north," he would say.

Just before he was to leave for work that night there was a knock at the door. Two men.

"Health inspectors," said one. "Checking for smallpox."

Lim Sam bolted.

He didn't know how long or how far he ran. He lay on the side of a ditch, legs aching, chest pounding. Terrified. He heard the approach of dogs. Voices yelling in the blackness, "We'll get the dirty Chink." He slid slowly down to the bottom of the ditch, grasped his knees in his arms and closed his eyes. A tiny woman, far, far away, was waving.

They kept him locked up in a barn until they decided what could be done with him. A doctor examined him and diagnosed leprosy of either the tuberculoid or lepromatous type, he couldn't be certain. They sent him under custody to Victoria where Dr. George L. Milne, the city's medical health officer, examined him and confirmed lepromatous leprosy. Mr. Theodore Davie, the Member of Parliament for Vancouver Island, asked the Victoria City Council whether Lim Sam could be confined at the lazaretto on D'Arcy Island if the provincial government reimbursed the city for the costs. The council agreed. On September 4, Labour Day, of 1892, the steamer *Alert* took Lim Sam to D'Arcy Island.

That was almost seven years ago. Mr. Benjamin Bailey, the sanitation officer, accompanied him, along with Alderman Joshua Holland and Dr. Milne. Mr. Bailey told him that he would be looked after. That he didn't need to worry any more about food, clothing or shelter. That was all taken care of.

"You need not worry any more, lad," he said. "We will look after you."

Benjamin Bailey was a big, jolly man with laughing, bottomless, glass-like eyes, and whiskers. He saw every action, every decision as an improvement over whatever had gone before. No matter what. He took his job very seriously, making sure his "unfortunates" got their supplies every three months. Sometimes he brought the doctor with him and sometimes a group of city officials.

After loading the supplies, the little steamer left Victoria harbour about 9:00 A.M. As the *Alert* chugged its way along the shore, past Ogden, Finlayson, Clover, Harling and Gonzales points, the young city and the community of Oak Bay appeared not unlike Hong Kong Island as it had been three years ago when Lim Sam first saw it from aboard the junk that took him there. Since being captured he had cried for many days. His soul, torn from within, was displayed mockingly before him, together with his wife and son who seemed so small in his memory. He saw his mother cut the umbilical cord of his younger brother and die. He saw the oozing sores on his father's face. His mind was numb, unresponsive to his perceptions. The rocky shoreline moved past him in a parade of cold monotony. At Ten Mile Point the *Alert* entered Haro Strait for the course to D'Arcy Island. Drizzle, then rain. The sea was grey and flat, hissing accusations borrowed from the beginning of life. Leper! Unclean! Holiday fires burned along the beach at Cordova Bay. The captain stayed fairly close to shore as far as Cowichan Head, then turned easterly for the remaining short run to the island.

The lazaretto was located in a small bay on the eastern side of the island. Fine gravel mantled the gently sloping beach so that, with the day's rising tide and calm seas, the *Alert* could be beached bow on— with an anchor aft to hold her stern into the swell. At other times she would tie up to an anchored buoy from which supplies and people were rowed ashore. The building above the beach was rectangular, about 48 feet long and 15 feet wide, and oriented in an east-to-west direction. It was divided into six cubicles, or cells, all of them opening onto a common veranda upon which stood seven men who had come out to view the arrival of the steamer.

"Hello, John," called Alderman Holland to one of the men who had come down to the beach. His name was Nap Sing, but like everyone else here, he answered to the name John.

"Missa Holland. You bring another."

Joshua Holland was in his early 30s, tall, straight, beardless, but with a full black moustache. It was he who, as chairman of the Sanitation Committee, took charge of the "leper problem," overseeing the construction of the building as well as arranging for regular, quarterly supplies and moving the first five men onto the island.

"Where he come from?"

"Nanaimo. Coal miner," Holland said in his usual clipped manner.

While Benjamin Bailey and the steamer's crew unloaded the supplies, Holland and Dr. Milne went up to the building to inspect the quarters. In every cubicle there was a fireplace, wood stove, bed, table and chair. Each had a window, and a door opening onto the veranda. The walls were insulated with shavings and the beds had straw mattresses. The two men were surprised to find most things in their place, although clothes were scattered about because there was no place to hang them. Holland wrote himself a reminder to send out some clothes-hooks on the next supply visit.

One of the things that impressed the visitors most was the garden. The men had managed to clear about three-quarters of an acre of land where they were growing potatoes, onions, lettuce, carrots and other vegetables. They even had plans for a small orchard. The doctor was quite amazed given that, at the time of their delivery to the island, the men had been in a state of profound depression and misery. They had cried and wailed during the entire trip and upon arriving, they just sat on the beach, in desperate silence. And now, only a little over three months later, they were seen to be a working community of co-operating, seemingly contented human beings.

"Remarkable," said Benjamin Bailey.

Dr. Milne wanted to examine each of the residents to see if their conditions had changed since late May when he last visited the island. He first examined Nap Sing, a little man who, when he was young, had studied to become a Taoist monk; however, he had decided that he couldn't afford the total rejection of the material world and that an interlude in Canada would increase his meagre financial resources. Since its first appearance the disease had progressed rapidly until he had no fingers on either hand, few remaining toes and his lips and nose were swollen and twisted.

"Well, it doesn't seem to be any worse, John," said the doctor. "Always keep a close watch on the ulcers on the bottoms of your feet. Clean anything out of them. Wash your feet often, it'll help keep the infection down, and for goodness sake, wear those overshoes we give you. They'll prevent further injury. You can't feel anything John, so you have to watch for things. Get the others to help you. Get them to tell you if they see anything."

Lim Sam watched the doctor go from one patient's cubicle to another until he had examined them all. Drained of any feelings about anything, his gaze wandered aimlessly about the tiny community of which he was now a part. He got to his feet and ambled slowly over to the smaller of the two buildings where he was told he would live, in a cubicle beside a man called Oung Moi Toy. He went inside and sat on the bed, his hands between his knees.

Before he left, Alderman Holland took orders: a mirror, a razor, one dozen chickens, a pig and a few handkerchiefs. As the *Alert* pulled away the rain stopped and the sun came out. Steam rose from the drying roofs of the buildings. To the west, across Cordova Channel the billowing black clouds began to break up and blue sky spread over the Malahat Range on Vancouver Island.

The tide whispers a song. The wind makes me remember. At the end of the sky you wait for me, yet I can not come.

Escape from where? No ships stop at the place with no name, and I can not swim. A thirst for gold brought me here. Still, I can not come.

My guilt is heavy, my sickness bad. I see you alone and I feel sad. I can never come.

Never.

CHAPTER ONE

Alone:
Without the camp

> *All the days wherein the plague shall be in him*
> *he shall be defiled; he is unclean: he shall dwell*
> *alone; without the camp shall his habitation be.*
> *Leviticus 13:46.*

LEPROSY.[3] ONE OF the oldest and most feared scourges of the human experience. Most of its victims exist neither in records nor memories. Its ravages rent families asunder, established the bottom rung of global poverty and created a mythology which until only recently elicited feelings of fear and loathing. In General Lewis Wallace's novel *Ben Hur* the disease is portrayed as the ultimate cruelty, far worse than death. Throughout the gruesome tautology of *Leviticus* 13, God is portrayed as the author of the socio-economic purgatory in which, for centuries, the banished victims of the disease lived in squalor and filth.[4] During the Dark and Middle Ages the Christian church enthusiastically supported this principle through imposing an astonishing variety of cruelties and thus fostered the stigma, which in some quarters remains today. Until this century medical science turned away from the disease, most of its practitioners afraid of getting too close, or, through fear of association, of losing other patients. Indeed, it wasn't until 1874 that the Norwegian physician Gerhard Henrik Armauer Hansen identified the bacillus that caused it—*Mycobacterium leprae*. Although most commonly known as leprosy, its formal medical name is "Hansen's disease."

It seems that the geographical origin of leprosy lay in Asia, possibly within the Indus River Valley of India, from which it was introduced to western civilizations, first by the returning army of Alexander the Great in 326 B.C. and later by Roman armies. Although the disease spread widely throughout Europe and elsewhere, during medieval times its prevalence was undoubtedly exaggerated through misdiagnosis and confusion with other diseases such as bubonic plague, psoriasis and syphilis, all of which show similarly pronounced visible effects. In *Leviticus* and other parts of the *Old Testament* the word translated as leprosy was the Hebrew *zara'ath* which today is believed to have encompassed a wide variety of diseases which may or may not have included leprosy as it is known today.

Indeed, the biblical descriptions of the disease do not include loss of sensation or missing fingers and toes, the primary indicators of leprosy. In the *New Testament* the Greek word *lepra* was used and it is more likely to have been what we call leprosy than the word zara'ath. Whatever the case, a scourge it was, causing most societies to condemn its victims to a life of poverty and suffering, a life not very different from that suffered today by the victims of AIDS, the "modern-day leprosy,"[5] throughout central Africa.

Insofar as those who contracted leprosy were generally malnourished and lived in crowded and unhygienic conditions, the disease tended to be concentrated within non-technological societies, much as it is today. The map of current global leprosy distribution shows that the greatest concentration of the disease is in the Third World—India, Brazil, Madagascar and states in central, western and parts of eastern Africa, Indonesia, New Guinea and the southwest Pacific. According to the World Health Organization, in 1998 there were an estimated 6,000,000 cases in the world (prevalence), while the number of new cases detected each year (incidence) is about half a million. This annual rate of incidence has not declined significantly over the past several years, suggesting that unknown carriers and methods of transmission of the bacillus may be important.[6] There are about 5,000 cases in the United States with about 200 new cases reported annually, and fewer than 200 known cases in Canada.

Chaulmoogra oil, a derivative of the seeds of the genus *Hydnocarpus* of the Indian plum family, either by oral application or injection, was for many years the established treatment of leprosy. Its first clinical use was in Bengal in 1853, following which this treatment became widespread until near the end of the first half of the 20th century. Since 1946 the sulfone drug dapsone and more recently rifampin and clofazimine have greatly reduced the global prevalence of the disease. Leprosy is now curable to the extent that a patient can be cleansed of the bacillus and surgery can reduce the disfigurement. However, the destruction of nerves remains, resulting in loss of feeling, most importantly the sensation of pain.

The bacillus *Mycobacterium leprae* is a rod-shaped organism similar to that which causes tuberculosis. Although the means of infection remains uncertain, it is thought that the bacteria are taken into the body through inhalation or prolonged and frequent skin contact, commonly with family members. Other forms of transmission may be through mosquitoes and other insect carriers and by contact with armadillos, the only other known mammalian host, of which some 15% are thought to be infected with *M. leprae* in Texas and Louisiana. Some soils are also believed to harbour the bacillus. Leprosy is one of the least infectious diseases known; about 95% of the world's population is immune, the remaining 5% contract the disease through intimate family contact; children are most susceptible in areas where nutrition and hygiene are poor.

There are two forms of the disease, each representing end-members of a continuum. At one end is the so-called *tuberculoid* form, which is localized, caused by comparatively few bacilli and characterized by hard, insensitive nodules, or tubercles, that form on the skin. In the more generalized *lepromatous* form, enormous numbers of bacilli occur in the deep layers of the skin from which they spread widely through the lymphatic channels and along trunk nerves to damage peripheral nerves near cooler surface areas of the hands, feet, face and ears. Actively multiplying *M. leprae* causes damage only where the body is cooler than the core body temperature. For example, a common nerve trunk impairment is that of the ulnar nerve, lying just below the skin at the elbow which leads to clawing of the fourth and fifth fingers and loss of feeling in the hands, whereas the median nerve is not damaged because it lies deep in the muscles where it is warm. The air-cooled mucous membranes of the nose, mouth and throat may be invaded. In these cases the moist lining of the nose swells, blocking the passage of air and causing the sufferer to become a mouth-breather. This results in the cooling of the larynx followed by swelling of its soft tissues. Breathing becomes difficult; before treatment was available a common cause of death was suffocation.

The eyes can be infected in one or more of several ways, including damage to three of the cranial nerves that control exclusively the motor muscles attached to the eye. Two other ways are the anaesthetizing of the cool cornea and iris so that the victim is unaware of dust and grit getting onto the eye, and the paralysis of the nerves leading to the muscles of the eyelid which permit it to blink. Damage to the cornea is manifested by the appearance of thick, white scar tissue covering the eye; loss of lubrication afforded by blinking leads to drying of the surface of the cornea with consequent cracking and ulceration. In either case the victim becomes completely blind.

Nasal cartilage commonly is affected, leading to septal collapse and the so-called "saddle nose" deformity. The classic disfigurements of leprosy also include the "leonine facies," a lion-like appearance with thickened, nodulous skin. The loss of sensation that accompanies the destruction of nerves may result in unnoticed injuries and ulcers, in turn leading to secondary infections and the erosion of fingers and toes. In severe cases nerve damage leads to muscular atrophy and, through consequent loss of calcium, progressive internal reduction of the bones of the fingers and toes. The majority of sufferers have symptoms of both tuberculoid and lepromatous end-member types, a condition known as "borderline" leprosy; depending upon which end-member is dominant, cases are classified as either borderline tuberculoid or borderline lepromatous.

The development of leprosy is slow, the incubation period ranging from two to 40 years. An infected child may not show symptoms of the disease until adulthood when, from the first appearance of a spot on the skin, the disease progresses with increased disability and deformity. Although they suffer occasionally from fever, and may die from suffocation as a direct consequence of the disease without proper medical attention, victims most commonly succumb to secondary infections arising from injuries, including ulcerated skin caused by sustained pressure as when sleeping or standing for long periods. Pulmonary tuberculosis and pneumonia are common causes of death.

Lepers feel no pain in the infected parts of the body. Even those cured of the disease feel no pain. In *Pain: The Gift Nobody Wants,* by Dr. Paul Brand and Philip Yancey, the absence of the sensation of pain in the hands, feet and face is shown to be an enormous disability. During many years of working with leprosy sufferers in India, Dr. Brand pioneered corrective surgical techniques and developed measures for the management of bodies, which were denied the warning mechanism of pain. Although his colleagues argued that he was wasting his time, he found lasting solutions to many puzzling aspects of the disease, one of which was the assertion by some that a victim's fingers or toes had *suddenly* fallen off.

It was known that fingers and toes could lose flesh and bone through erosion, injury or infection, but it was unlikely that this would happen suddenly, even though such claims were part of the mythology of the disease. However, Dr. Brand took the claims seriously enough to investigate their veracity. He discovered that a victim can indeed suddenly lose one or more fingers or toes overnight, but the loss was due to rats. Without the sensation of pain, a sleeping leper with infected and senseless digits was an easy target for nocturnal rats, which could feed on the diseased flesh without the victim's notice. Presumably, some victims may have bled to death.

Other manifestations of the absence of pain included infections arising from ulcerated bedsores, and cases where men were seen walking about, without limping, on ulcerated feet whose bare bone was in contact with the ground. Thorns, rocks, or bits of broken glass could be lodged deeply in a foot, completely unnoticed.

A commonly unrealized effect of the destruction of the peripheral nerves is a loss of any sense of where the feet are in relation to the rest of the body. It is not dissimilar to the effects of freezing of the jaw and mouth during a visit to the dentist. One loses perception of the position of tongue and cheeks relative to one's teeth and it is difficult to drink because one has no sense of lips against a container. Although the inner ear triggers muscle-controlling nerves in the feet to maintain balance, the victims of Hansen's disease need to rely much more upon their eyes to place their feet in the correct position for walking and standing; otherwise they have no sense of where their feet are. The same is true for their hands. When they grasp something, it is their eyes, which tell them if the operation is successful. If blind, the leper is literally lost in his world.

In the Victoria of 1891 other diseases besides leprosy occasionally were a serious threat to the young city. These included smallpox, of which there were a number of small outbreaks and a comparatively significant one in 1893 during which some 40 cases occurred,[7] diphtheria, tuberculosis and, rarely, bubonic plague, among others. None of these, however, elicited such extraordinary measures of isolation.

Just what was known by the medical profession of Victoria about Hansen's disease at the time the D'Arcy Island lazaretto was established? A perusal of medical texts in use at that time indicates that doctors had a good understanding of the pathology and symptoms of the two forms of the disease, tuberculoid and "anaesthetic" (lepromatous), and the bacillus that caused them. Other aspects, such as mode of transmission, were speculative, except it was widely recognized that close and prolonged contact with a carrier, usually a family member, was important. As to contagiousness, most doctors, including the well-known Canadian physician Sir William Osler, believed that complete isolation of infected individuals was necessary. In 1897 the International Congress on Leprosy at Berlin recommended that "in all countries in which there are centres of leprosy, or in which the disease extends, isolation is the best means of preventing its propagation."[8]

Despite these assertions by prominent medical authorities, Dr. J.S. Helmcken, a respected Victoria surgeon and politician, testified before the Royal Commission on Chinese Immigration in 1885 that "according to the best medical authorities, leprosy is not considered a contagious or infectious disease ... I do not know that it is necessary a leper should be locked up ..." Also, in October of 1906, Dr. Felix Montizambert, Director General of Public Health for the dominion government, made several statements concerning the low degree of danger to the public from leprosy, including the following: "I would sooner be in a leper ward than one containing a case of common influenza. I can become infected with the latter, not the former."[9]

It seems that for the period during which the City of Victoria bore responsibility for the lazaretto, the medical profession had no common understanding of the degree to which the public was at risk. Moreover, in none of the texts examined was there any mention of treatment for infections through injury as a consequence of nerve and muscle damage. Dr. George H. Duncan, Victoria's medical health officer, succinctly expressed his ignorance of the disease and its treatment when, to a Victoria *Daily Colonist* reporter on June 16, 1895, he said, "Just now, the best we can do is to isolate the poor sufferers, for the protection of the public, and make their few weeks or months here as comfortable as we can. We are, as to treatment, just where we were a score of centuries ago."

As to modern attitudes toward the disease Dr. Paul Brand, who recently visited China to give lectures to their Leprosy Service, wrote, "In that country, in spite of the fact that they have a very good program for detecting the earliest cases of leprosy, and giving them the modern treatment which results in complete cure of the disease, yet at the same time, throughout the country there are hundreds of leprosy colonies with high walls in which the old deformed patients who have already lost fingers and feet and are blind are kept in isolation. They are provided with food and shelter, but nobody will touch them. There is a higher level of total segregation of this type of patient than I have seen anywhere else I've been."[10] It seems, therefore, that old fears still linger in some parts of the world.

Toward the end of the 19th century, when chaulmoogra oil was widely used as a treatment for Hansen's disease in the leprosaria of India, Hawaii, Norway and at the famous lazaretto at Carville, Louisiana, Dr. F.P. Foster wrote, "While the evidence does not show that the remedy is absolutely curative, many believe that it exerts a favourable effect on the course of the disease. Under its influence all the symptoms may diminish or even entirely disappear for a time and the patient show marked improvement in weight and general condition."[11] The side effects of its use included pronounced nausea when given orally, and pain, because of its high viscosity, when injected. Although the oil was difficult to acquire because of the scarcity of the plant from which it was derived, and the remoteness of the areas in India and Malaysia where it grew, when the federal government assumed responsibility for D'Arcy Island in 1906, it immediately established a program of medical treatment including the use of chaulmoogra oil; since prior to 1900, it had also been used at Tracadie, New Brunswick, Canada's only other leprosarium. Thus, had the City of Victoria chosen to provide medical care, chaulmoogra oil was available.

As HE SAT staring through the holes in his overshoes at his bloody feet, Lim Sam recalled how the disease had slowly progressed through his body as though he were a meal for some silent parasite. Since he had arrived on the island his hands continued to be affected so that his fingers became senseless and shrunken through internal dissolution of the bone. While cooking and lighting his fire he often burnt himself with the result that his right hand was twisted and scorched. His feet were the next to go, but very slowly. First it was his right foot that gradually lost any sensation. At some time he cut himself severely but the injury went unnoticed for many weeks. Finally, the infection became so obvious that Nap Sing and Sim Lee undertook to clean the wound and apply some natural remedies they had concocted from plants collected from the surrounding forest. Eventually the infection subsided and shortly after that his two friends were dead, one from suffocation and the other from tuberculosis.

During the cold and wet winters he would lie in his bed until hunger or his bowels forced him to move. Large bedsores covered his thighs and these too would become infected unless he cleaned and bandaged them, which sometimes he did and at other times he didn't. Most often they would heal themselves, only to reappear somewhere else. If they grew on his back he would go to his friends to ask for help in treating them. But now his friends were dead and most of the others were too sick to be of any help.

His face and eyes were the last to be assaulted. His nose had collapsed, his lips thickened and his face took on the loathsome leonine facies so common to sufferers of leprosy. His features appeared as a distorted melange of misshapen pieces of flesh, somehow glued together to form a whole surrounding his eyes. He had lost the sight in one eye because he no longer blinked; the eye had cracked open and infection had swarmed in.

As he lay in his bed, afraid to move because he could barely see and walk, and afraid to lie still because of spreading bedsores and growing weakness, he wondered if the life-taking storm had finally arrived. He knew that nobody would come to help. Even though the small steamer had arrived, he knew that there was little chance that anything would change. At length he had roused himself and walked down to the beach to sit on a log and watch the seamen carry the supplies ashore.

He stared down at his boots and saw the blood that had oozed from his feet. His friends had died and soon, so would he. He would be hauled away into the bush behind the garden, there to be buried by people just barely more alive than himself. He would be put in a coffin supplied by the city. Large rocks would be placed around the coffin while smaller ones and soil would be piled on top. Someone might pound in a stake near his head. He would be dead in a place that was nowhere.

Leprosy appears to be unique in western cultures insofar as it carries a stigma that has remained unchanged through time. Whereas other diseases such as bubonic plague, syphilis and many others are all unchangingly loathsome, their associated stigmas have evolved to the point where, today, little remains. Leprosy, on the other hand, until only recently, remained associated with filth, poverty, ignorance and sin. Also, in other cultures, such as those of Asia, the same stigma appeared. It is interesting to note that by the early half of the 16th century in Europe, the disease had virtually vanished but it reappeared in the 19th century as a consequence of imperialism when soldiers returned home; the same stigma also reappeared. What is it about leprosy that caused such an immutable stigma and mythology?[12]

The subject of stigma has been for many years, and continues to be, a favourite of sociologists and leprologists. As applied to leprosy, everything from the miserable admonitions of *Leviticus* to socio-economic environments has been invoked as constant causes for the persistence of the stigma attached to the disease. The leprophobia that spread throughout British Columbia and, more intensively, the United States, during the latter half of the 19th century is likely to have been due as much to the rebirth of ancient biblical beliefs as it was a product of direct observation and consequent fear of association. The reaction of the observer throughout history has been the same—revulsion and horror toward the victim and the consequent assignment of blame for being afflicted. Whereas other diseases, far more deadly and debilitating, are broadly accepted as a part of life, none elicits dread as does leprosy. Why?

Perhaps the immutable stigma of leprosy has to do with our feelings of horror over incurable disfigurement by a slow, creeping death, coupled with the lingering fear that if we come into contact with a leper, we will become one ourselves. We remain victims of the mythology of the disease. Our fingers and toes will fall off and our faces will contort into a hideousness that only banishment can hide. And perhaps, deep in our psyche, buried beneath all of the trappings of modern attitudes and beliefs, lies the soul-numbing fear that leprosy is God's inevitable punishment for committing sin. Before the Day of Judgement arrives, it is His bottom line. It's the ultimate boogeyman whose image has remained unchanged for thousands of years.

Moreover, leprosy is one of the very few diseases whose victims have been given a name. Lepers. The name perpetuates the stigma. If he's a leper, then, by definition, he is unclean and lives in filth and squalor and, during the late 19th century, he came from alien cultures such as China. In this way, at least in much of western North America, leprosy became a corollary of race and contributed to the justification of anti-Chinese prejudice.

"It is, of course, unfair to saddle the cities with the cost of the support of these Chinese lepers. They cannot be considered citizens of British Columbia in any sense of the term. If British Columbians had their way there would be no Chinese in the province."

Victoria *Daily Colonist*, November 17, 1891

CHAPTER TWO

Island
of death

THE HISTORY OF the D'Arcy Island leper colony may be divided into two distinctly different periods: first from its establishment by the City of Victoria in May of 1891 until 1906,[13] after which the dominion government assumed responsibility and managed the facility until 1924. Of these two periods it is the first 15 years which is the main focus of this book.

On March 4, 1891, one F.W. Foster, a local justice of the peace and self-appointed city watchdog, notified the City Council of Victoria, British Columbia, that "Chinese lepers were allowed to go about the City and

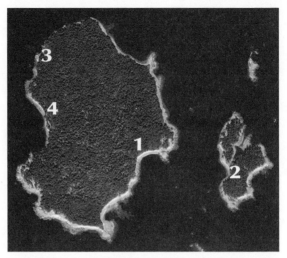

Vertical aerial photograph (BC 7751#234) showing the locations of facilities constructed for the D'Arcy Island lazaretto. 1. Lazaretto 1891-1906; 2. Lazaretto 1907-1917; 3. Guardian's residence 1907-1924; 4. Lazaretto 1917-1924. (B.C. Government photo).

View southward from D'Arcy Island to Little D'Arcy Island. The modern house is on the approximate site of the detention buildings from 1907 to 1917. Part of the concrete foundation of the lazaretto is incorporated in the house.

that the public health was endangered thereby and requesting that steps be taken to prevent such diseased persons from wandering about the City."[14] This information set in motion the establishment of Canada's second leper colony on nearby D'Arcy Island.

D'Arcy Island, named after John D'Arcy, a mate on H.M.S. *Herald* during her visit to British Columbia in 1846,[15] is located about one nautical mile south of Sidney Island in Haro Strait which separates the San Juan Islands (U.S.A.) from southern Vancouver Island. The roughly square-shaped island, which was first surveyed for the provincial government in May of 1890 by George Morrison, is approximately one kilometre long and wide, embracing an area of some 82 hectares (202 acres) and densely mantled by Douglas fir, arbutus, alder, western maple, poplar, willows and shore pine. Salal, Nootka roses and reed grass, the latter in boggy areas, are common. Bedrock consists of Paleozoic lava,[16] which forms the rugged, angular shoreline and is intermittently exposed throughout the interior, where it is covered by stony and sandy glacial clay, or till. All slopes are gentle, rising to about 24 metres at the north end of the island from which elevations gradually decline toward the south and somewhat more steeply to the east. At a few places there are grassy bogs which dry in summer and at other times of the year supply water for small seasonal streams draining the eastern slope. These bogs are due to a shallow water table into

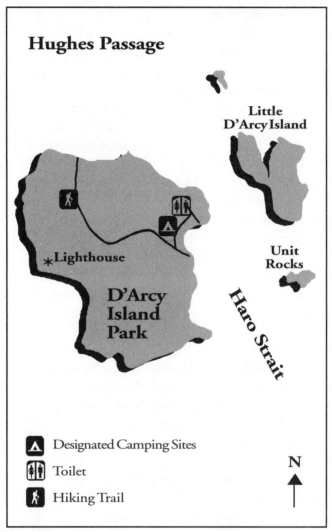

Hughes Passage

Little D'Arcy Island

Unit Rocks

*Lighthouse

D'Arcy Island Park

Haro Strait

▲ Designated Camping Sites

🚻 Toilet

🚶 Hiking Trail

N

B.C. Parks map of D'Arcy Island showing recreational facilities.

which at least two wells were dug during the latter history of the colony.

Deer, racoon and a variety of smaller animals have been seen on the island as have various shore birds, gulls, eagles, ravens and the ubiquitous Pacific crow. The few pocket beaches yield clams and mussels and not far off the island's western shore live Dungeness crab. The surrounding waters of Haro Strait are cold; maximum summer surface temperatures reach 15 degrees Celsius.[17] Tides, flooding north and ebbing south, can reach three knots and, at times of maximum flow, strong tide rips occur which, when acted upon by northwesterly or southeasterly winds, can result in steep, chaotic waves. The island is currently included within British Columbia's marine park system; nearby Little D'Arcy Island, off its eastern shore, is privately owned.

The lazaretto was constructed by the Victoria municipal government above a gravel beach fronting a shallow bay[18] in the middle of the eastern shore of the island.[19] Above the log-strewn upper beach the surface is flat, with several broad areas of medium-density forest covering stony and pebbly clay and sandy glacial soil. According to the *Daily Colonist* of May 15, 1891, the lazaretto was to be established within 100 feet of fresh water. Although there is no stream, there is a boggy area with several pools of fresh water about 250 feet north of the building site. There is no evidence of a well. The location of the original building, constructed in 1891

Piece of a
headboard
from an
iron-frame
bed.

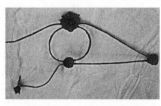

Detail of the
headboard.

Fruit trees, probably descendant from the original orchard.

and burned to the ground in 1907, is evidenced by two rows of stone post-footings, the front row consisting of seven, carefully placed rocks, their upper surfaces flat and parallel with the ground surface, each six feet apart and on a straight line bearing 270 degrees; the back row is largely grass-covered with only four such footings observable. Three concentrations of scorched, collapsed chimney firebrick and numerous broken fragments of ceramic kitchenware are evident, and rusted and corroded parts of beds, metal wood-stove doors and door hinges are widely scattered about the surrounding grounds. Stunted fruit trees, possibly survivors from an original orchard, occur in parallel rows not far from where the original building was located.

Evidence of at least five graves is provided by mounds and stone rings, clearly man-made and consisting of angular blocks of rock surrounding an elevated mound within which other rocks and soil were placed. While three of these mounds are several metres behind the building site, two others are very close to one another and to the building's location. Those farthest from the building site tend to be large enough to have served as multiple graves; the two close by are much smaller.

The view the residents had was toward the southeast where, in the far distance, they could see Discovery and Chatham islands off the Oak Bay waterfront. If they climbed the low hill immediately east of the main building they could see Ten Mile Point in Oak Bay, as well as the

Remains of the woodshed and workshop for the caretaker's cottage.

distant American San Juan Islands and nearby Little D'Arcy Island, the latter only about 400 metres away.

About one kilometre across the island on its western shore are buildings constructed after 1906 when the dominion government assumed responsibility for the facility. The caretaker's house, built in 1907-1908,[20] the remains of the workshop, cellar and woodshed, constructed in 1909-1910, and the orchard are north of the lighthouse; to the south are two concrete foundations, each 5.8 m by 9.8 m, built as detention houses in 1917 and 1918. A short distance inland from the two small house foundations are remains of pipes for water supply from a dug well, as well as two pits which may have served as latrines. A narrow ditch extending seaward to the beach from close to one of the pits probably facilitated drainage. About 50 metres south of the southernmost of the two house foundations is a natural bench with an elliptical depression, bordered on one side by a parallel, narrow mound; this could be a grave site.

Between 1906 and 1917 patients sent to the colony were housed in two buildings constructed by the Department of Public Works on Little D'Arcy Island;[21] the concrete remains of these buildings have been incorporated into the structure of a modern house.[22] Interestingly, no documents or newspaper accounts refer to Little D'Arcy Island as the site of the colony between 1906 and 1917; it seems that in the minds of officials and the press the term "D'Arcy Island" included its smaller neighbour.

Victoria City Council, 1891. Back row, left to right: F.G. Richards, C.E. Renouf, Jno. Coughlan, Joshua Holland (Chairman of the Sanitation Committee), W.J. Dowler (City Clerk), H.A. Munn. Front row, left to right: J. Robertson, A.J. Smith, John Grant (Mayor), W.D. McKillican, Jos. Hunter.

At the time of the establishment of the lazaretto, the community of Victoria was 48 years old. A city council, divided into several committees, serving three wards, managed an infrastructure including police and fire departments, harbour authority, hospitals, cemeteries, and construction and maintenance departments, all of which were supported by a resource-based economy depending on logging, coal mining and fishing. The 1891 city council consisted of the mayor, John Grant, and nine aldermen: F.G. Richards, C.E. Renouf, Jno. Coughlan, Joshua Holland, H.A. Munn, J. Robertson,

A.J. Smith, W.D. McKillican and Jos. Hunter. Municipal business was managed by the city clerk, W.J. Dowler. The most important committee as far as the lazaretto was concerned was the Sanitation Committee, headed by Alderman Holland with Munn and Renouf as members. Benjamin Bailey was the sanitation officer. At that time the annual municipal expenditures, totalling just over $1,000,000, served a population of 22,500, mainly Caucasians, but also including some 2,080 people of Chinese origin.[23] A significant number of itinerant natives from the several nearby bands also contributed to the cultural mix.

Chinese immigrants first arrived in Victoria from San Francisco in 1858, at the beginning of the Fraser River gold rush. By 1860 it was estimated that the combined Chinese population of Vancouver Island and British Columbia, then separate colonies, was about 7,000 people, almost entirely men. Most of these, mainly peasants, came from South China, the region between Canton and Hong Kong, and, in collusion with some ship-owners, were supplied for the building of the Canadian Pacific Railway, to fish canneries and to mining companies by notoriously unscrupulous labour brokers such as Syme, Muir and Co. and Tait and Co.[24] Because of rural poverty and political instability in China, peasant immigration again increased during the 1870s and 1880s, largely in response to the continuing need for cheap labour to build the C.P.R. Other industries such as mining and fish-packing also attracted Chinese labour, as did the demand for domestic servants including cooks, gardeners and laundrymen.[25] By finding employment overseas, an immigrant could send money home to support relatives and hope to return home eventually with enough cash to live in comparative comfort.

As with any immigration of large numbers of aliens into an established population of a differing culture, Chinese immigration into Canada, mainly to British Columbia, inevitably aroused feelings of prejudice. Due to the arrival of greater and greater numbers, Canadian immigration policy as of 1885 required a $50 "entry," "head" or "poll" tax for each Chinese immigrant before he was admitted to the country. In response to further pressure, again mainly from British Columbia, in 1901 the head tax was increased to $100, infuriating some politicians who wanted it increased to $500. In 1902 the dominion government responded by appointing the Royal Commission on Chinese and Japanese Immigration which concluded that the Asians were "unfit for full citizenship ... obnoxious to a free community and dangerous to the state."[26] In 1903 the head tax was raised to $500 with the desired result: the number of immigrants dropped substantially. Soon, immigration increased again and on July 1, 1923, known to the Chinese as "Humiliation Day," the Chinese Immigration Act was replaced by legislation which suspended Chinese immigration almost entirely.[27] In

1947 this legislation was repealed and the Chinese gained the right to vote nationally and provincially. However, it wasn't until 1967 that Canadian immigration policy became "non-racial."

Anti-Chinese attitudes expressed by those who lived in the Greater Victoria area differed from those residents of the mainland of British Columbia during the late decades of the 19th century.[28] Whereas the latter's prejudice against the Chinese, and later the Japanese as well, bordered on outright hatred, as expressed by a staggering array of egregious atrocities, the feeling of the Caucasian population of southern Vancouver Island was one of reluctant but condescending tolerance.[29] True, there were many instances of prejudice among local merchants and politicians, and Victoria's newspapers carried strong anti-Chinese articles on a regular basis; however, their degree of prejudice was far less than that seen elsewhere in British Columbia. The reason for this difference may be found in the contrasting socio-economic environments of Vancouver and Victoria.

Vancouver was young, brash, burgeoning and populated by a wide variety of Caucasians from many countries, including the western United States where anti-Chinese sentiment was very strong. Victoria, on the other hand, had been established by a wealthy, educated, landed gentry of dominantly Scottish and English origins, who, over several decades of imperialism, had become accustomed to living among peoples of different origins; this allowed for the development of patronizing attitudes to what they believed to be inferior races and cultures. Many of Victoria's Chinese merchants who had come north from San Francisco in the late 1850s were also wealthy and contributed substantially to both Chinese and white charities and the construction of hospitals and other public works. In contrast, Vancouver's smaller Chinatown lacked this strong financial and philanthropic underpinning.

As in other communities, some of Victoria's citizenry took advantage of the vices the Chinese had to offer, such as gambling, opium dens and brothels, the evils of which were regularly, but not too often, railed against by the city fathers, who had one eye on the next election and the other on that great gateway in the sky. Also, "pagan" Chinese New Year and funeral spectacles delighted the population. Thus, although racial prejudice in Victoria was evident and occasionally strong, it was at a lesser degree than that commonly expressed in Vancouver and throughout the interior of the province. With but one exception,[30] the attitude of the Victoria newspapers toward the lepers of D'Arcy Island was one of sympathy, albeit restrained. It is clear that had the victims of leprosy depended upon the people of the mainland interior they would have fared much worse.

It was within this environment of racial prejudice that five Chinese men, found to have leprosy, were discovered living in a shack behind the Kwong Wo &

Co. store on Fisgard Street between Douglas and Government.[31] Although a few previous cases of leprosy among the Chinese population of Victoria had been known,[32] the attitude of the city was that there was little threat to the white community because the Chinese kept largely to themselves and that the Celestial[33] community should take responsibility for their care and deportation back to China. It was not until the discovery of the five men that the city government felt itself compelled to take serious action. How it was that these men had escaped discovery is puzzling since routine inspections for smallpox and other diseases were frequently conducted throughout the Chinese community. Also, the fact that they were all living together suggests that the Chinese community wanted both to isolate them and to protect them from discovery by the health authorities.

Following confirmation of Foster's March 4 report to city council by Dr. G.L. Milne, Victoria's medical health officer, and Dr. A.C. Smith of Newcastle, New Brunswick, who was in charge of the lazaretto at Tracadie, and who had been asked by the dominion government to confirm the diagnosis of leprosy and report on the prevalence of the disease throughout British Columbia, the city council acted swiftly. It authorized the sanitary committee to recommend that the city clerk communicate with the provincial government, requesting that D'Arcy Island be set aside for "municipal purposes."[34] In June of 1886 the island had been leased to one J.H.

G.L. Milne, M.D.
Victoria Medical Health
Officer, 1891-1892.

Benjamin Bailey.
Victoria Sanitary Officer,
1891-1893.

Garrett for a period of ten years at $12 per year.[35] Presumably the provincial government terminated the lease, because on April 22, 1891, the sanitary committee reported to council that their request had been granted.[36] Ten days later the *Daily Colonist* noted that the city's Board of Aldermen visited D'Arcy Island where they looked upon it "as a very good place for the erection of the *garbage crematory*" (author's emphasis).[37] Clearly the city fathers felt the need for secrecy, fearing that knowledge of lepers about in the city would alarm the populace. They were probably right, and the fact that the victims were Chinese would not have helped.

The secrecy ended on May 5 when the rival newspaper, the *Daily Times*, published an article entitled "Where the Lepers Will Live" in which it described plans for their incarceration, accommodation and care. The degree to which the Caucasian citizenry was alarmed over news of the necessity to construct such a facility is difficult to assess for the only reference to it was an utterly indecipherable comment in the *Daily Colonist* of May 15, 1891: "The fact of the city endeavouring to secure D'Arcy Island for sanitary purposes has attracted *a greater or less amount of attention to this subject* ...." (author's emphasis). As for the Celestial community, who undoubtedly knew of the situation, some idea of their concern for their countrymen is given in a *Daily Colonist* article which describes the efforts of Alderman Joshua Holland to raise money from the Chinese community for the support of the lepers; the results of his initial efforts amounted to $40 and some rice.[38]

On May 13 the *Daily Times* reported that the steamer *Alert* was to leave that day for the island with men and materials to construct the buildings designed by the well-known architect John Teague under the supervision of a Mr. Northcott. In addition to the building, a 60-foot pole was erected on a nearby hill from which a distress flag could be flown in the event of an emergency. It was believed that this would attract the attention of any ships passing through Haro Strait and city council was to request the press to publish a notice to master mariners to watch for this distress signal. No such notice was ever published.

On May 20 the five Chinese men were taken aboard the steamer *Alert*, under the command of Captain Clark, and transported to D'Arcy Island in the company of Alderman Holland, Sanitary Officer Benjamin Bailey, Dr. A.C. Smith of New Brunswick, Sergeant Thomas Walker of the Victoria Police and Ah Wing, an interpreter. The five men were:

Sim Lee, age 52, who had resided in America for nine years, most of that time in Victoria. He had a wife and child in China.

Ng Chung, age 39. He also had a wife and child in China. As the *Alert* was about to leave he attempted to cut his throat but was prevented from doing so by Sergeant Walker.

Chin You, age 34. Single.

Nap Sing, age 41. He had been in Victoria for four years and had a wife and 12-year old son in China.[39]

Ah Chee, age 32. He had been a Victoria resident for four years.

This list of the island's first residents is in order of increasing deformity and development of the disease.[40] Sim Lee's symptoms were such that he could have escaped casual inspection, whereas the others ranged from deformities of the fingers and hands through massive swellings and tubercle development on the face, to loss of fingers and toes, and cracked, ulcerated and scaly skin. Most of them had no feeling in their hands, feet and faces, some noses were twisted and had collapsed, eyebrows were gone and lips swollen. Ultimately, some would become blind. During the trip to the island Dr. Smith is reported to have "selected several pieces of scaling flesh from their hands and bodies for microscopical examination";[41] this appears to have been a favourite practice among visiting physicians as reported in other press articles throughout the following 15 years. How it benefited the individual physician or the medical profession is unknown but it must have humiliated the sufferers.

In addition to providing accommodation, city council arranged that food, clothing, and other commodities, occasionally including opium, would be delivered to the island's inhabitants every three months. Food consisted of rice, potatoes, sugar, flour, meal, bacon, salt pork, tea, dried fish and other items as the residents requested. Cutlery, fishing gear, axes and gardening tools also were provided. Although it was the intention to re-supply the colony quarterly, this interval was occasionally extended to as much as four months. That these men feared what was in store for them is evidenced by the actions of Ng Chung, described above, and of two others: one who, rather than being sent to the island, committed suicide by taking poison in 1893,[42] and the other, Lee Sing, possibly from Nanaimo, who escaped deportation to the island in August of 1892 and was never seen again.[43] It should be said, however, that, given the poor economic conditions of the time and the slim chances of employment for many of the immigrants, particularly the leprous Chinese, even among their own kind, such arrangements were better than they otherwise could have expected. At the very least they would die not of starvation or exposure, but rather from disease and medical neglect.

When the first five of the island's residents arrived there was a rumour that another man had previously been placed on the island and that he had either died or escaped. On May 22 a return visit by several people, including Fire Chief Thomas Deasey, failed to find any trace of such a person. In a Victoria *Times Colonist* article published on September 2, 1979, Alice Tomlinson described a case in which, in 1890, a Chinese man (presumably suffering from leprosy) had been taken to the island; three months later the "health inspector reported that his one and only patient was missing ..." Although the same account is given in a 1985 article by Ilma C. Salazar Gourley, this apparently popular story cannot be substantiated by contemporary accounts. If indeed the city authorities had done such a thing, to so isolate a man without shelter or other support, it would have been tantamount to murder.

Following the victims' incarceration on the island, the shack on Fisgard Street in which they had lived was burned to the ground by the fire department. Throughout the spring and early summer the island's residents were able to clear about three-quarters of an acre of land and plant potatoes, onions, lettuce and other vegetables. A pig and a dozen chickens, which they had requested on a late June visit by Bailey, Holland and Milne, were promptly delivered, together with a razor, a looking-glass and a few handkerchiefs. The pig was undoubtedly used for land clearing and to provide fertilizer for the garden. Thus it was that despite their great handicaps, the lepers were initially able to function well and, according to Benjamin Bailey's reports, seemed contented.

It should be noted that, "Dr. Milne says that one of the Victoria Chinamen is not a leper, and should be released to liberty."[44] There is no evidence that anyone was released from the island, and if the report was true, it was possibly Sim Lee who was the unaffected man. It would be tragic indeed if, by ignoring the doctor's observation, a man's life and liberty were taken from him through callous indifference on the part of Victoria City Council. However, as the article was about negotiations between authorities in Victoria and Vancouver with regard to the latter's wish to send two leprous Chinese to the island, the reporter may have misunderstood the doctor's statement as applying to one of the original five Victoria lepers; one of the two Vancouver men was found to have syphilis rather than leprosy and was released.

News of the lazaretto quickly spread to other cities such as Nanaimo and Vancouver, each of which had leprous residents their councils wanted to be rid of. Throughout the fall and winter of 1891 negotiations with these cities led to the removal of one man from Vancouver.[45] A Nanaimo man, possibly named Lee Sing, seems to have escaped deportation to the island;[46] a telegram sent by Dr. A. C. Smith, dated May 21, 1891, suggested that he was "probably killed by his fellow countrymen." After a considerable amount of haggling between Victoria and Vancouver it was ultimately decided that Vancouver would repay Victoria on a *pro rata* basis rather than manage the maintenance of its own lepers. Both cities agreed to pressure the dominion government jointly to take responsibility for the facility, and the Vancouver Board of Health planned to "forward all bills in connection with the matter to the C.P.R. who brought the lepers to Vancouver and left them there."[47]

This photograph may be of the first six residents of D'Arcy Island, possibly taken in 1892. The two men sitting in the middle, each of whom shows the effects of the tuberculoid form of the disease, are possibly Ng Chung (right) and Chin You. The oldest, sitting on the left in the back row, would be Sim Lee who, together with the remainder of the group, suffered from the lepromatous form of leprosy. The man in the front row, right, appears to be the tallest and thus could be Oung Moi Toy, the "New York leper." Each individual was told to prominently display his infirmity, even to the point of removing his shoes. Their reaction to this order is seen in their faces.

Such efforts were initially unsuccessful; however, much later, steamship companies, including the C.P.R., were required to pay deportation costs for lepers they brought to Canada.[48]

The case of the Vancouver man is bizarre. It seems that two Chinese lepers were deported from the United States where they had been living in New York. They were transported in quarantine, probably in a crate, by the C.P.R. to Vancouver from which they were to return to China, but no ship would take them. Upon hearing of their arrival the Vancouver authorities decided to send them back whence they had come. However, they only got as far as Swift Current, Saskatchewan, when the dominion government stepped in and returned them by train to Vancouver, not wishing to annoy the Americans. At first the C.P.R. confined them to a guarded shack while Vancouver authorities squabbled with Ottawa as to who should assume responsibility for them. Ottawa's refusal to co-operate prompted the city authorities to release the two men, who wandered about the city and were apparently shunned by their countrymen. Following furious outcries by local politicians and the press the two were returned to the shack where they were voluntarily supplied with food by generous citizens. When it was discovered that one of them did not have leprosy at all, but rather syphilis, which he had contracted in New York, he was given a new set of clothes and released.

A close-up view of two of the residents.

However, it was confirmed by health officials in Vancouver and Victoria that the other man, whose name was Oung Moi Toy, did have leprosy in addition to syphilis and henceforth became known to Vancouver and Victoria authorities and the press as the "New York leper." He was described as stout, with a fair command of English. He could also read and write.[49] He wanted to be returned to Hong Kong where he had a wife and a much beloved 80-year-old mother but, for lack of sympathy and a quarantine ship, was sent to D'Arcy

Island near the end of December of 1891. Oung Moi Toy was also described as a gambler, a liar and a supply-hoarding bully[50] and was transported to the island in a crate.[51] The authorities in Vancouver had agreed to supply and construct living accommodation for him and to pay his share of the quarterly supplies. His building's dimensions were 12 by 16 feet, divided into two rooms, one for living and the other for tools and stores.[52] Thus, by the end of 1891 there were six men living on D'Arcy Island.

It is probable that sometime during 1892 or 1893 another man from Vancouver arrived on the island. This is supported by a document, which states that, "in September 1893 the City of Vancouver put in a claim for the expenses of two lepers sent by it to the island."[53] The year was probably 1892 because it is known that the population of the colony had increased by one, to seven, by the end of that year.[54] The name of this man is unknown; however, he may have been Lim Sam, the main character of the Prologue and the resident who died in a fire on the island in 1899.

STILL SITTING ON his log, Lim Sam let his memories wander slowly across the seven years since his arrival. He had stayed in his cabin for a long time until hunger forced him to seek food and other supplies stored in one of the cubicles in the main building. Nap Sing and Sim Lee helped him carry things back to his cabin. The other cubicle in the building was occupied by Oung Moi Toy whom everyone hated and feared. Sim Lee, in his quiet, gentle voice said that they would probably kill Oung Moi Toy some day. Oung Moi Toy was a big brute of a man who swore and swaggered about the colony and ordered the others to do his bidding or suffer being beaten up. He hoarded the best and largest amount of the supplies for himself and threatened anyone who challenged him. Gradually, however, fear of Oung Moi Toy subsided for it became apparent that the disease was rapidly weakening him to the point where the growls and threats from his vicious mouth were of little consequence.

Nap Sing and Lim Sam had become good friends. On warm summer evenings they would often talk well into the early hours of the morning. They told one another of their lives in China and how it was that they ended up on this island.

"Who reported you?" asked Lim Sam when Nap Sing told him about being discovered with four others in the shack behind the Kwong Wo & Co. store.

"I don't know. It doesn't matter now anyway. I'll die soon. It would be nice if they would send me home but they say they can't find a quarantine ship. They probably haven't even tried."

Although he was only in his early 40s Nap Sing looked much older. The disease had grossly deformed his face, hands and feet and he had lost most of his fingers and toes, probably to nocturnal rats that ate away the senseless flesh while he slept. The rats had probably come to the island on one or more of the quarterly supply runs, or perhaps on some of the Japanese fishing boats that occasionally came by to trade food supplies for some of the colony's opium.

As the months and seasons passed, the tiny community developed a subtle internal governmental structure; the residents co-operated to ensure that water was carried up from the bog, the latrine pit had enough loose soil for covering and sufficient firewood had been cut for warmth and cooking. Job sharing and rotation among the residents allowed time for maintaining the large garden and tending to the chickens and pig. When one of the residents died or a newcomer arrived, the community was able to absorb the change with equanimity.

A death was never a problem. The dead man had to be carried or dragged sufficiently far from the buildings so that his ghost would not bother the surviving residents. The favoured place was toward the bog where a shallow depression could be dug, around which stones were placed in a ring. Someone would bring down one of the coffins from the storage room in the main building. The coffin was placed in the centre of the ring and the corpse put in the coffin, which was then covered with soil and stones. Nap Sing would find a broken branch and, with Lim Sam's help, pound it into the ground near the head. Easy. No fuss. No talk.

Lim Sam remembered the time when Nap Sing first spoke of his son. "He would be about 16 now," he said, his voice a whisper, distant and sad. By then the disease had found its way into his larynx, causing him to some-times gasp for air. "He's probably wanting to come to Canada too. There's nothing for him in China and only hatred here but at least he can earn some kind of a living."

A week later Nap Sing died, of suffocation.

The photographs of the colony are not identified as to when they were taken, but clearly they fall into two distinct groups. Those showing the building and individual victims are of remarkably high quality, and were probably taken in 1897 during a visit to the colony by Dr. Ernest Hall and John Nelson.[55] On the other hand the two group photographs do not include the same individuals shown in the other photographs, are

TABLE I	Year	Expenditure	Revenue	Year	Expenditure	Revenue
Municipal Expenditures & Revenues Re D'Arcy Island Lazaretto 1891 to 1904	1891	1134.36		1898	892.21	465.30
	1892	994.10		1899	1116.82	244.56
	1893	577.91	1217.03 [a]	1900	905.05	544.27
	1894	1724.12	269.47 [b]	1901	774.60	520.70
	1895	1105.67	1462.90	1902	796.13	192.37
	1896	835.12	465.33	1903	712.02	6225.35 [c]
	1897	947.59	431.83	1904	790.23	754.83

a. Includes: $1000 from the dominion government; $190.23 from the City of Vancouver; $26.80 from the provincial government.
b. Revenues are mainly refunds from other municipalities.
c. Provincial government assumes expenses as of October, 1903. This amount was reimbursed to the City of Victoria.

TABLE II
Annual Breakdown of Costs

An example of an annual breakdown of costs, dated December 31, 1897, is as follows:[57]

Clothing 106.80
Provisions 567.27
Furniture, crockery, etc. 81.32
Hire of steamer 120.00
Interpreter 7.50
Garden seeds 2.00
Cartridges 16.00
Tobacco 14.50
Ambulance 1.50
Coffins 16.25
Sanitary Inspector expenses 13.45
Hauling 1.00
Total: $947.59

The listing of cartridges implies that the residents had weapons of some kind, presumably for game.

of distinctly poorer quality, and show there were six residents at the time. Because there were only four years when the year-end total number of residents was six— 1891, 1893, 1899 and 1905 (see Table III) and given the poor quality of the photos, which were taken by a portable camera invented by George Eastman only six or seven years earlier, it seems reasonable to speculate that the people shown in the group photos were the island's first residents.

The cost of establishing and maintaining the lazaretto on D'Arcy Island for its first year, in 1891 dollars, amounted to $1,134.36.[56] Because other communities wished to take advantage of the situation, Victoria City Council insisted that they pay their share of the costs. It wasn't long before this argument expanded to include the dominion government; because it operated a leprosarium at Tracadie, New Brunswick, under the authority of the Quarantine Act as administered by the Department of Agriculture, city council assumed Ottawa should adopt the same responsibility for D'Arcy Island. Although the dominion government reluctantly contributed limited amounts of money to the D'Arcy Island operation, the Victoria city fathers were most disappointed to learn that Parliament lacked their enthusiasm for the idea and for several years the city directed its arguments and pleas toward a far-away deaf ear.

Reports by Sanitary Officer Bailey[58] and those of the medical health officers make it difficult to assess the

TABLE III	Year	Arrivals	Deaths	Year End Total Residents
Population History of D'Arcy Island: 1891 to 1907	1891	6	0	6
	1892	1	0	7
	1893	1	2	6
	1894	4*	1	8
	1895	2	1	9
	1896	0	2(?)	7
	1897	2	1	8
	1898	0(1?)	1(2?)	7
	1899	1	2	6
	1900	0	1	5
	1901	1	2	4
	1902	0	0	4
	1903	0	2	2
	1904	3	0	5
	1905	1	0	6
	1906	2	0	8
	1907	0	0	8
				Deported

*One of these men escaped.

Total permanent residents: 23.
Total deaths: 15.
Total deported to China: 8

progress of the disease on the residents due to inconsistencies in reporting and a lack of details on their condition at times of visits by authorities or the press. For example, on January 11, 1892, in a letter to Victoria City Council, Bailey wrote, "The one sent from Vancouver is in a very bad condition—his face and neck are very much inflamed and sore." The next day the *Daily Colonist*, reporting on the same visit, claimed, "The Vancouver man was much improved in appearance..." In no reports, either annual reports of the medical or sanitary officers to city council or articles in the press, are there descriptions of the infirmities of the residents or details of the progress of the disease. All accounts are generalized: "they are much worse," or "the plague in the case of two of the Victoria party has so advanced that they can no longer work, and they seem to be rapidly approaching their end."[59] There was no indication of why they were much worse, or what was killing them—it certainly wasn't leprosy because one does not normally die from the disease; one dies from infection and/or secondary disease enabled by the weakened condition of the sufferer.

During 1892 the seven men were visited four times by Mr. Bailey, Dr. Milne and, toward the end of the year, Dr. G.H. Duncan, who replaced Dr. Milne as medical health officer. As early as February three of the original five residents were no longer able to work, and one of these was insane as a consequence of a tree falling

TABLE IV
D'Arcy Island
Residents: 1891
to 1906

Name	Arrived	Died	Returned to China
Sim Lee	1891		
Ng Chung	1891		
Chin You	1891		
Nap Sing	1891		
Ah Chee	1891		
Oung Moi Toy	1891	1895	
Unknown (Lim Sam ?)	1892	1899	
Alexander (Charles ?) Sundy	1893	1893	
? Sing	1894		
Ah Lung	1894		
Unknown (miner)	1894	1894?	
Unknown (escaped)	1894		
Chin Wah Yuen	1894 ?		
Lang Nung	1894 ?		
Unknown	1895 ?		
Ah Sing	1895		
Lung Hing (Steveston leper)	1897?		
Unknown (Vancouver)	1897		
Unknown (Jack)?	1898		
Unknown	1899		1907
Unknown	1901		1907
Unknown (Ah Jack-Vancouver)	1904		1907
Ng Chun (Vancouver)	1904		1907
Unknown (Victoria)	1904		1907
Unknown	1905		1907
Unknown	1906		1907
Unknown	1906		1907

on his head —"almost every night he goes roaming about in the woods shouting and singing ..."[60] During the late summer a house had nearly been completed for Lee Sing before he escaped deportation to the island. By August, 1892, the colony had managed to increase its chicken population to 20 and its number of pigs to nine. At the end of 1892 the authorities ceased using the steamer *Alert*; thereafter, one of the several vessels named *Sadie*, owned by the Victoria Tug Company, was used to transport visitors and supplies to the island.

In February of 1893 another man, in very poor condition, was taken to the island, which would have brought the population to eight. However, the *Daily Colonist* reported that a recent death on the island reduced the total residents to six.[61] If the press report was correct, another man had died and his passing went unrecorded. This is an example of the difficulty of ascertaining how many residents there were at any given time. Table III, showing the population history, represents an attempt to combine population information supplied by the press and the annual reports of the sanitary and medical health officers. This is particularly difficult for the years 1895 and 1896 when no reports were submitted on D'Arcy Island by either the medical health officer or the sanitary officer; moreover, there were very few press reports for 1896. Although many of the residents' names are known, rarely do accounts of deaths provide names, making it impossible in most cases to know when a certain individual died. Also, because there are no death records of any of the island's residents, in the majority of cases causes of deaths are unknown; indeed, in British Columbia there are no records of any Chinese deaths prior to 1897. Not surprisingly, there are no coroner's reports for any deaths on the island. In the mind of officialdom, these people simply did not exist.

Table IV shows when recorded individuals arrived on D'Arcy Island between 1891 and 1906. All of the people whose names are known, as well as those with unknown names, appear in the text. With the exception of 1894 the number of arrivals is in agreement with those shown in Table III. In 1894 there are three arrivals more than are shown in the population history table. Also, the total number of arrivals differs by three in the two tables. Insofar as Table III is reasonably accurate and controlled by the Year End Total Residents column, in most cases given in annual reports of the medical and sanitary officers, the listing in Table IV for the year 1894 is suspect. Two possible explanations are inaccurate reporting by the press and different names being used by the same individuals.

CHAPTER THREE

Moans of a lost soul

ON MARCH 19, 1893, the only Caucasian resident was delivered to the island. Alexander Sundy,[62] a German-Russian and an early resident of Victoria, contracted the disease either at Alert Bay on Cormorant Island off northern Vancouver Island, or at Port Simpson, north of Prince Rupert.[63] His disease was at a very advanced stage, and one report claimed that he was so shunned by his Chinese companions that, when he died several weeks later, they refused to bury his body until they were threatened with having their supplies withheld.[64] The reasons for this behaviour are not given. It may have been that his condition was so bad that the others didn't want to go near him for fear of their own conditions becoming worse, or perhaps that it was distasteful to them to help a white man. There were claims that Alexander Sundy contracted the disease in the Chinese quarter of Victoria where he resided.[65] If indeed he had been a resident of Victoria's Chinatown he may have been known and despised by some of his Chinese companions prior to their incarceration. Since this was the first year of deaths on the island, one might think that this would merit some comment in the year-end annual reports of the sanitary and medical health officers; in fact, there is no mention of D'Arcy Island in either report for the year 1893.

LIM SAM REMEMBERED Alexander Sundy well. He remembered watching as Mr. Bailey and an assistant carried what was left of him up the beach and laid it on the grass in front of the veranda. He was a pitiful sight with barely any flesh on his bones. He lay gasping and puking on the ground while Mr. Bailey and Captain Clark scouted out accommodation for him.

"Look at the disgusting scum." It was Ah Chee, the hatred in his voice unmistakable.

"Why is he a disgusting scum?" asked Lim Sam.

"He's a bloodsucker. All of Chinatown hates him.

He used extortion to get us to pay so we wouldn't get beaten up or our businesses wrecked. His gang used to wander about, beating people up in full sight of the police who watched and did nothing. That rotten Sergeant Walker was his buddy. The two of them ran brothels together and sometimes they would kidnap women from our brothels. I hope it was one of ours that gave him leprosy. It would serve the miserable insect right."

Lim Sam looked down upon the broken and pathetic sight at his feet. "He's no threat to anyone now."

"Yeah, well he's not going to get any help from any of us. As far as we're concerned he might just as well die right there."

After Alexander Sundy had been carried up into an empty cabin, Lim Sam stood in the doorway, looking at him. He remembered his father being taken away and wondered if he had ever come to look like this. Will I look like this?

Somewhere out in the forest behind the building came the screaming giggles of Chin You who had had a tree fall on his head a while back. Since then his mind had been reduced to that of a child and his great joy was in singing two lines from a song that he had heard Australian passengers singing on his journey from China.

"Washing Malitla, Washing Malitla
Who come Washing Malitla with me?"

Over and over and over again he sang in the only
English he knew. At the end of several repetitions he
would shriek in delight and go dancing off into the
forest. Once he had fallen into the latrine pit and had to
be extracted by Lim Sam and others, taken down to the
beach and washed in the surf, all the while shouting
"Washing Malitla, Washing ..."

As Lim Sam gazed upon Alexander Sundy he realized
that he had no feelings for the man at all, good or bad.
He felt utterly indifferent to his race and the disease that
was sucking the life from him. If no one else cared, why
should he? He too was going to die here and nobody
would care about him either. Still, something made him
continue to stare at the creature on the bed. There was
something about that tangle of bones and wrinkled,
paper-thin skin that fascinated him. The genitals were
unshrunken and hugely occupied the space of his crotch
as though they were the last bastion of life.

Over the next few weeks Lim Sam took upon
himself the chore of looking after Sundy. Cooking for
him and helping him to eat what little he could,
helping him to the bucket where he relieved himself
and emptying it afterwards, bringing him water. All the
while no words were spoken. Sundy would cough and
spit and occasionally groan. None of the others helped
and for a while they ignored Lim Sam, all except Sim
Lee who would smile and gently put his hand on Lim
Sam's shoulder when he passed.

Six weeks after he arrived on the island, Alexander Sundy died of pneumonia. It happened the day before a supply visit. When Mr. Bailey heard that the residents refused to bury him he threatened to withhold their supplies. Lim Sam and Sim Lee agreed to do the job. They dragged the emaciated body into the edge of the forest bordering the garden and buried it in a shallow grave in the same way as they did the others. Knowing that Sundy was probably a Christian, Sim Lee fashioned a cross out of branches and pushed it into the dirt beside the grave.

There were six left.

During July and August of 1894 a correspondence occurred among Emma M. Barrett of Port Townsend, Washington, Reverend E.D. McLaren of St. Andrew's Presbyterian Church in Victoria and Theodore Davie, Attorney General of British Columbia, regarding the wishes of a Mrs. Hansel who had offered to go to D'Arcy Island to "immolate herself [sic] for the benefit of the unfortunate lepers ..."[66]

The attorney general turned the request down: "... it does seem to us that the devoted services which Mrs. Hansel is prepared to render might be applied to a cause still more in the interests and for the benefit of mankind ... . they [the lepers] have been well attended and it would seem that the misery of their lot can hardly be alleviated by placing a guardian among them."[67] The reaction of Reverend McLaren to this refusal was one of fury; in addition to referring to the damage that such a decision would create among the Christian missions throughout China, he threatened to "write up the whole case for the eastern papers and appeal to the Christian public of Ontario for the money refused by the municipal and provincial governments here."[68] The attorney general's apparent belief that the lepers were not a part of mankind, and the prohibitive cost of providing accommodation and support for a lone woman on the island, undoubtedly greatly influenced his decision, but why the attorney general was involved at all is puzzling—at this point the provincial government had nothing to do with the operation of the lazaretto.

With the arrival of four more sufferers in August and September 1894, the population on the island reached nine. One was named Sing and another Ah Lung. The third, a miner from Tranquille Creek near Kamloops, was "shipped from Vancouver, boxed up in a crate." His toes had "fallen off and he was a shocking sight."[69] The fourth was diagnosed with leprosy by Dr. Duncan; however, his friends in Victoria vigorously protested the diagnosis, making his removal to the island difficult. The diagnosis was later confirmed by a Dr. Lang who, at the request of the Chinese community, visited the island in October. In his annual report to council, Dr.

Duncan made reference to two other men, one of whom avoided deportation by taking poison and another who escaped after being taken to the island.

This latter may have been the one who protested the diagnosis and who, according to Dr. Duncan, escaped, possibly with the assistance of his friends. A more appealing variation on this incident, but one which should be considered apocryphal, was reported by the *Daily Colonist* of January 15, 1905, in which it was alleged that the man was rescued by his bride of only three months who sailed to the island in a sloop to effect his escape. Whatever the means, this is one of only two documented cases of a successful escape from D'Arcy Island during its use as a lazaretto. The other was Arthur Davis who, with the help of family and friends, escaped from the island on August 10, 1920.[70] Another escape attempt was described by Alice Tomlinson;[71] a man was said to have been carried by the tide to the shore of James Island from which he was returned to the lazaretto, but there is no support for this story.

Therefore, with the one successful escape, by the end of 1894 there were eight occupants of the lazaretto. With the construction of the six new buildings in October of 1894, as well as the partly completed one mentioned earlier, the community was beginning to take on the appearance of a tiny village. Also, it is probable that several shacks and lean-tos had been built, together with storage space in addition to that at the west end of the original main building. With Oung Moi Toy's cabin and the main building, the number of known structures was nine. This might suggest a scene of untidy chaos; however, in all reports by the sanitary officers, only neatness and order were observed, both individually and collectively.[72]

This was in contrast to Chinatown in Victoria, which was commonly described by the media as foul-smelling, disease-threatening and dirty. In the annual reports of the medical health officers, the district was often the subject of much concern, particularly in regard to garbage disposal and the use of human faeces in the growing of vegetables, which were sold to the public. Although such fertilizer was undoubtedly used on D'Arcy Island, along with that provided by the pigs and chickens, and although their method of garbage management is unknown, it appears that the residents organized their environment in accordance with civilized practice. Likewise, their vegetable garden and orchard, in which they took great pride, was commonly described in glowing terms, such as "would be the envy of almost any of the local gardeners."[73]

In May of 1895, Oung Moi Toy, the "New York leper" was dead. One month later a *Daily Colonist* reporter accompanied Dr. Duncan on one of the quarterly visits to the island. The result was a lengthy article providing many details on the conditions and lives of the inhabitants, and entitled "The Island of Death." At the time of this visit there were eight men on the island, one of whom, a recent arrival, would run through the woods and cry all night. "By 'm' by he not mind so much," said one of the residents to the reporter. In further describing their reaction to being imprisoned the reporter wrote: "When first taken to the lazaretto he realises the infinite horror of his position and for the time is a frenzied madman. Then comes the hysterical stage, and afterwards the dull, deadened, hopeless waiting for death."[74] Among the residents were Nip (Nap) Sing and Fong Sim Lei (probably Sim Lee),[75] two of the original five from Victoria, as well as Chin Wah Yuen and Lang Nung, this last from Manitoba. Another may have been Lim Sam, who, at the time of his death in 1899, was described by the *Daily Colonist* as one of the first to be sent to the island.[76] All of these men were in an advanced stage of the disease, having lost their fingers and toes, and some had suffered severe deformity to their faces. An interesting aspect of this and other reports was that no one individual among them would admit that he had leprosy, each explaining away his symptoms as a consequence of poison ivy or frostbite or some other cause; however, each insisted that it was leprosy that afflicted his companions. It is probable that this attitude was an expression of their remaining hope that they would be taken off the island if their assertions were found to be true. Since each individual's symptoms were different in type and stage of development from those of his companions, it was not difficult for a man to convince himself that his ailment was something other than leprosy.

Dr. Duncan appears to have lacked the sensitivity of his predecessor and successors and may have taken his duties as medical health officer for the city less seriously than they did. Indeed, for the years 1893 and 1895 he made no mention of D'Arcy Island in his annual reports to council and, in 1896, failed to submit a report at all. This latter was no doubt due to his resignation on September 28, 1896, which appears to have been somewhat acrimonious. During the June 1895 visit to the island Dr. Duncan took photographs of the residents who understandably were most reluctant but he was able to persuade them by falsely saying that photos were needed in order to determine how many of them were fit to return to China. The reporter may have been somewhat contemptuous of the doctor when reporting that he took "minute notes on the special characteristics of each case for the edification of his professional brethren."[77] There was no description of medical ministry, of applying bandages to ulcerated limbs, or of administering chaulmoogra oil.[78]

In October another leper, Ah Sing, was brought to the island, bringing the population to nine. About one month later two doctors from H.M.S. *Royal Arthur*, who were said to have much experience with leprosy in the Orient, are said to have expressed the view that "the lazaretto on D'Arcy Island is superior to anything they

R.L. Fraser, M.D.
Victoria Medical Health Officer, 1897-1901.

The original lazaretto building. This was taken during a supply run, probably in 1897 during the visit of Dr. Ernest Hall and John Nelson. The bifurcated tree just beyond the left (west) end of the building can be compared with the tree shown in the 1999 photograph (see page 142). Could the man sitting on the log be Lim Sam?

had seen."[79] However, they may have been impressed mostly with its overall appearance and operational procedures; they could not have been impressed with the medical care, for there was none. Again, the year-end annual reports of Dr. Duncan and M.J. Conlin, the sanitary officer, gave no mention of D'Arcy Island for the year 1895 and, at the end of the following year, during which two residents must have died, no statements were submitted by either of these men. Apart from a report of a supply run in May of 1896 by Sanitary Officer R. Chipchase, the next mention of the lazaretto was on February 23, 1897, when the *Daily Colonist* described the visit to the island by Aldermen Partridge, Hall and Stewart in the company of Sanitary Officer Chipchase,[80] and Drs. Fraser and Richardson, the former replacing Dr. Duncan as medical health officer. The article about the visit in the *Daily Colonist* included the statement: "No change is apparent in the condition of the seven inhabitants of the little colony, and all are in excellent spirits."[81]

In September of that year, Lung Hing, a man from Steveston, was brought to the island without prior consultation with Victoria authorities. He was described as being in the very early stages of the disease and thus was of considerable help to the other, more infirm residents. In December another sufferer from Vancouver was added to the population. Dr. R.L. Fraser's December 1897 annual report was curt: "I visited D'Arcy Island

Close-up of some of the residents standing on the veranda of the main building. This was probably taken in 1897 during the visit of Dr. Ernest Hall and John Nelson. The man in the right foreground is probably Sanitary Officer Chipchase.

four times during the year. There are eight lepers, all Chinese, at present on the island. Two new cases were admitted and one death occurred during the year."[82] The death must have occurred prior to May of 1897; its circumstances and who died are unknown.

In 1898 Dr. Ernest Hall and John Nelson, in the *Dominion Medical Monthly and Ontario Medical Journal*, published observations gathered during a visit to D'Arcy Island.[83] This report is among the most valuable sources of information on the island's inhabitants. Although the article was published in June of 1898, it does not say what year the visit occurred. It is probable, however, that the occasion was in May of 1897: "It was one of those delightful mornings in May, when ... ."[84] It is unlikely that it would have taken only one month to make the visit, write the article and get it published, so it is reasonable to assume that the visit occurred at least one year before the article appeared.

At the time of their visit there were seven inhabitants. The sanitary officer was informed that a man had died shortly before the visit, prompting Dr. Hall and Mr. Nelson to write: "for back there amid the wild shrubbery just bursting into bloom, with the waves singing their requiem, lies the poor yellow tenement [sic] out of which the troubled and lonely spirits have at last struggled into rest and peace."[85] At some point, one of the residents noticed that the visiting party included a woman, no doubt the first he had seen for some months or even years. "Oh, laddee, laddee" he exclaimed, bowing before her. The following passage illustrates the compassion that Hall and Nelson felt: "Who may fathom the workings of his mind? Weeks had lengthened into months and months to years, and these again had dragged round their successive cycles, for while suffering may be the sacrament of life, it does not hasten its flight. In all these years who can tell what passionate yearnings he may have had for far Cathay, and for those days of his younger manhood sweet to the human heart? Whatever the colour of the skin, when arms of love encircled his neck, and the endearments of wife or sister or sweetheart or eastern mother gave to life a tenderness and charm. Little wonder that even the alien face of a white woman may have recalled to his poor mind a suggestion in his expression of wistful womanly sympathy of days long since dead."[86]

The residents had no objection to Dr. Hall taking samples of their scaly flesh for medical purposes; however, as on a previous occasion, they greatly resented having their photographs taken. Neither of the authors of the article appears to have understood the sensitivity of the residents nor their deeply felt shame. Moreover, they appear not to fully grasp the actual nature of the disease, as they said, "Their footwear is confined almost exclusively to overshoes, as many of them have lost some of their toes and their feet are too painful to enclose in shoes."[87] The oversized footwear was undoubtedly preferred because of swelling, not because of pain which they did not feel.

Another expression of compassion for the island's residents is contained in a letter, written in January of 1898, by Dr. Ernest B.C. Hanington, a Victoria physician, to Sir William Osler, Canada's most prominent medical figure. "There are eight lepers in British Columbia—neither the local or the dominion government will assume any responsibility concerning them, so they are kept on D'Arcy Island, in the Gulf

This man's fingers are shortened due to internal dissolution of bone and his right eyelid seems to have been affected by the disease.

of Georgia and looked after by the Corporation of Victoria. They have no medical treatment whatever. The City Health Officer, or the Sanitary Inspector, makes visits about every three months taking them supplies, and making a report of the number of deaths since his last visit. The poor devils make gardens and catch some fish; *as to how they die, no one knows* [author's emphasis]. Each man has a shack and I fancy that his chief recreation is taking note the progress of the disease. I have been to the island twice and it was a very painful experience. The wretched beings, some in the last stages of the disease and a few with only a few lesions, lined up on the beach and cried like children when we were leaving—I have never heard the moans of a lost soul, but since hearing those poor wretches saying good bye (or damning us, I don't know which) I have a faint idea of what they are like."[88]

This letter prompted Osler to write to the Minister of Agriculture asking for more information. The reply was that the dominion government was not responsible for D'Arcy Island. The minister forwarded Osler's and Hanington's letters to British Columbia's Senator William Templeman who then asked Dr. R.L. Fraser, Victoria's medical health officer, for more information. Part of Dr. Fraser's reply was as follows: "It is hard for me to believe that the complaint received by the Minister was from a medical man. I am strongly inclined to think that it was made by some meddlesome missionary, several of whom visited the island during the last year."[89]

In May of 1898 an article appeared in several coastal newspapers, including some in San Francisco, claiming that the D'Arcy Island colony was selling surplus vegetables to people in Vancouver. Dr. Fraser gave no credibility to these reports; however, Dr. Duncan, now Secretary of the Provincial Board of Health, was dispatched to the island to investigate. On May 5 the *Daily Colonist* said that he found the claims untrue and, in its last paragraph, stated, "There is nothing particularly new to report concerning the colony of lepers *beyond the fact of the death of one of the Victoria Chinamen* [author's emphasis]. There is only one recent patient who came from Vancouver ..."[90] Three weeks later, on May 24, the *Daily Colonist,* in the account of a supply run said, "One of the lepers who came from Westminster [New Westminster?] died three weeks ago leaving now but seven unfortunates in the lazaretto." Accepting these reports at face value indicates that two people died within a few days of one another, though the *Daily Colonist* may have been confused over whether it was a Victoria or Vancouver (New Westminster) man who died.

In the fall of 1898, believing that quarterly visits were insufficient, Dr. Fraser managed to persuade the Victoria City Council to contract a Captain Johnson of Sidney to undertake visits to the colony every two weeks, to bring supplies as necessary and to report his observations to the

Could this be Lim Sam? He has lost the use of his right hand.

medical health officer. In November, on another supply run, Mr. Chipchase and Dr. Fraser noted the poor condition of the residents and, in his annual report for 1898, the latter said, "There are seven patients, all Chinese on the island … . Only two of the lepers are now able to do any work and the disease is making rapid inroads on the strength of these two. All of the others are very feeble and almost helpless and it will only be a short time until all are unable to care for themselves. When that time arrives some provision for nursing and caring for these unfortunates must be made."[91] By February 1899 another had died, this one from Vancouver, possibly the man delivered to the island in late December 1897.[92] This brought the population to six.

On Thursday evening, June 15, 1899, the *Daily Colonist* reported that an "old and feeble Chinaman,"[93] Lim Sam,[94] was burned to death. Recent articles by Alice Tomlinson[95] and Ilma C. Salazar Gourley[96] assert that Lim Sam was a young man of 19. Despite a search of immigration records from 1889 to 1899, many of which are unreadable, as well as other potential sources, no evidence to support either claim was found. The photograph, probably taken in 1897, shows a young resident who could be Lim Sam. Alternatively he could be the old man shown earlier, sitting on a log.

The fire apparently damaged the east wing of the main building and another resident's face and hands were badly burned.[97] The *Daily Colonist* reporter speculated that "the fire was caused by the man who lost his life, he getting up during the night to fix his fire, and probably dropping a hot coal which he did not notice, returned to bed to be burned."[98] Dr. Fraser's story, which follows, is somewhat different and probably more reliable insofar as he visited the island shortly thereafter. Of course, the obvious questions come to mind: what caused the fire and was it accidental?

The weather that day was normal for the season, 18°C during the day and 8°C at night;[99] thus it was not too warm for a fire. The reporter stated that "Some boatmen passing the island last Thursday noticed the ruins ..." According to a 1979 *Daily Colonist* article, "The handful of residents in Cordova Bay saw a bright light on D'Arcy, just two miles off their own splendid beach. The light flickered, rose higher, and then dimmed to a soft glow."[100] Dr. Fraser's version of the incident stated that it "had been a bush fire, June 15, at night."[101] It seems therefore that the fire occurred on the night of June 15 and "the ruins" were seen by the passing boatmen on Friday, June 16. Apparently it took three days for Dr. Fraser to get to the island to investigate the reports of the boatmen. Incidentally, on the day of the fire Dr. Fraser had visited the colony on a supply run, and that evening he penned a statement: "There are six lepers here, but only one is able to do any work. And he will not assist his companions." He finished with: "The conditions are simply terrible."[102] Was he referring to the conditions of the patients or the state of the lazaretto as a whole? If the latter, then things must have deteriorated substantially since the visit of Hall and Nelson two years earlier.

The night was quite mild with no rain, and by inference, no thunderstorms, therefore no lightning strikes. People in Cordova Bay apparently saw the fire and were able to describe it so it would seem that the fire occurred in the early to mid evening, before people went to bed. Although the above-quoted speculation of the *Daily Colonist* reporter was not unreasonable, could it have been otherwise?

BY NOW THE sun was low in the western sky and from his vantage point on the log Lim Sam could no longer see it. The forest rimming the colony had become dark and stark against the deepening blue of the sky. Dr. Fraser and the *Sadie* had left a few hours ago and the only remaining able-bodied men among the residents had taken the quarterly supplies up to the storage shed. The approaching evening was warm with no wind. It had been so for several days and much effort had been needed to bring water from the bog to the garden. Only one or two were able to do any work and the others only light duties before they fell upon their beds, exhausted.

Gazing down at his torn overshoes and bleeding feet he pondered Sim Lee's recent death from tuberculosis. That quiet, gentle, intelligent man had been reduced to choking and drowning in his own spit. No help from anyone. He had put the flag up the pole several days before Sim Lee died but nobody came. Nobody ever came. He was the last of the originals, surviving for eight years at the place with no name, where nine others lay buried beneath the ever-encroaching blanket of salal. Sim Lee had been their leader, father and friend, and without him the colony had begun to disintegrate. Jobs were being neglected and the new arrivals knew nothing of helping out with the feeding and care of those who were helpless. He knew that he too would soon be helpless. Oozing ulcers covered his back, buttocks and thighs, the products of pressure sores and countless other unnoticed traumas. His limbs were swollen and senseless, he felt nothing. He felt no pain. His eyebrows were gone, his nose collapsed, his lips swollen and his eyelids no longer blinked—he would soon be blind.

Resting upon his elbows with his head hanging low beneath his shoulders, Lim Sam begins to hum a song remembered from his childhood. The tune rises and falls in a soulful monotony while he gently sways from side to side in time with the rhythm of his song. It's about a little boy named Ping who goes fishing with his family. They use ducks to dive for fish but the ducks can't swallow their prey because of tight rings placed around their necks. Ping's favourite duck is always late in returning to the boat for which the bird is smacked with a stick.

It is now dark. The others have returned to their cabins where they have lit their fires and begun to cook their evening meal. Lim Sam slowly rises from his day-long sit and moves with difficulty up the beach to his cabin at the east end of the building. Someone, he knows not who, has lit his fire for him. He stands before it, swaying back and forth, still humming his song. He stoops and with senseless stumps for fingers, picks up a piece of burning wood with both hands. He gazes at it for a moment, the flame searing his flesh. He turns and goes back outside, down the steps of the veranda and out onto the grassy meadow beside the building. He drops the burning charcoal into the brittle, dry grass. He stands looking down as the grass quickly ignites. The fire leaps into the dark night and spreads rapidly through the meadow and toward the building. In the centre of the inferno he sees a tiny figure waving. He walks toward it and kneels among the flames.[103]

On June 29, 1899, the *Daily Colonist* reported that "The new buildings were then erected—a great improvement on the old." This suggests that the original, fire-damaged six-cell building was destroyed and replaced by a new one, probably under the supervision of Dr. Fraser and Building Inspector W.W. Northcott.[104] The June 15 fire was not the only one to occur on the island that year.

On the evening of August 5, passing steamers reported that the entire wooded portion of the island was ablaze and the colony's buildings were threatened.[105] No further information is available as to that fire's cause, how it was extinguished or the consequent damage. That it may have been started by unwanted visitors is supported by a *Daily Colonist* report of unauthorized overnight visits to the island by Japanese fishermen. Also, it was alleged that, following each supply run, several white men would come to the island to trade opium for some of the residents' provisions. These visits were apparently observed by people living on the shore of Cordova Bay,[106] and it is possible that the August 5 fire was a consequence of one of these types of visits, as perhaps was the one that killed Lim Sam on June 15. Of course, it is also possible that the reported fire was on a different island entirely, such as nearby Little D'Arcy Island. The lack of any further information renders the initial report suspicious.

In his annual report to Victoria City Council on December 23, 1899, in addition to his report on the June 15 fire, Dr. Fraser said that the lazaretto "is in a truly deplorable condition. Only one man is comfortably able to work. Two of them are quite helpless, and depend for food, fire, nursing and attendance on the feeble efforts of the others. The time has now arrived when some steps must be taken to provide for the proper care of these unfortunates." Dr. Fraser's efforts to get more attention for the lepers, which included the twice-a-month visits of Captain Johnson, speak of a compassionate man who deeply felt the suffering of the residents of D'Arcy Island. From the moment he assumed the job of medical health officer, replacing the less sympathetic George Duncan, Fraser pushed hard for greater support for the residents through arguing that the dominion government should assume responsibility for their care.

Although Dr. Fraser's arguments were purely medical and humanitarian, they supported those of the city which were entirely financial and which had been repeatedly presented to an unsympathetic dominion government from the time the lazaretto was established. Because the leprosarium at Tracadie, New Brunswick, was operated by the dominion government, it seemed logical that D'Arcy Island also should be under its care. Despite previous reports to council and the press that all was well with the colony, reports that may have been soothing for a collective guilty conscience, Dr. Fraser's observations shed the light of truth on the real conditions of the lepers on the island. Yet it was not until the promulgation of the Leprosy Act in 1906 that the dominion government assumed responsibility for D'Arcy Island, after which its residents received daily medical treatment from a resident caretaker and, later, a nurse.

At the turn of the century the lazaretto contained six residents, the most recent of whom was delivered on December 28.[107] As reported by Captain Johnson following a visit to the island on January 17, sometime before that date another resident had died.[108] For the remainder of 1900 little is known about life on the island, but by the end of that year Dr. Fraser's annual report indicated that all five Chinese patients were helpless. Only one was able to do any work and he refused to assist the others. Again Fraser urged that something more needed to be done beyond "merely supplying food and clothing." Five months later there were only three men left, one of whom had lost his voice and wasn't expected to live much longer.[109] In late June of 1901, a 19-year-old man from Victoria was delivered to the island. That same year, Dr. Fraser resigned and was replaced by Dr. Herman Melchior Robertson who made his first visit to the lazaretto in November and, in his annual report, said that there were four patients, three of whom were utterly helpless and were being supported by the boy. He also insisted that the dominion government should take charge.

On May 30, 1902, another visit by a *Daily Colonist* reporter, accompanied by several city and Presbyterian church officials, resulted in a lengthy article, entitled "The Isle of the Unclean," describing the conditions of the lazaretto and the four residents.[110] One of the patients had expected to be taken off the island and put elsewhere and was profoundly disappointed to learn otherwise. Apparently he couldn't get along with the others and claimed that they hoarded food and other supplies; perhaps the social order had broken down. The condition of the others was poor indeed; one had symptoms of both the lepromatous and tuberculoid forms of the disease. This individual could only hobble about on his knees, pushing with fingerless hands which were so deformed, badly swollen and seemingly useless that Dr. Robertson offered to amputate one of them, believing it to be "dead" because it had no feeling and no working muscles. The man refused and said, "S'pose you cut him off, no can cook." While Dr. Robertson bandaged his hands,[111] the preacher and missionary talked to him, telling him St. Mark's story of Christ healing the lepers and generally advertising Christian values. The man responded by asking the missionary if he would write to his uncle in China and tell him to drive his wife from his house because he believed that it was from her that he got the disease in the first place. It seems that the efforts of the missionary and preacher were less than impressive. Besides, "He had his joss and he worshipped his joss."[112] One of the men displayed the leonine facies, his brows and lips thickened, giving him the appearance of a lion. Still another had bark-like scales over his face, hands, breast and feet. All had lost most of their fingers and toes, their mouths were agape, and their facial features twisted, swollen or collapsed.

All of the residents were living in the main building, the others not having been used for some time. The walls were said to be papered with old copies of the *Daily Colonist* as well as "old-time New Year's visiting cards in their glory of black characters on big red papers ... as remembrance of the New Year celebrations the lepers miss on their lonely isle." At the close of 1902 there remained four residents.

In February of 1903 another leper died, possibly under suspicious circumstances suggestive of murder.[113] At the end of that year Dr. Robertson's annual report indicated another must have died, leaving the population at two. Of these he said "one has reached the chronic stage while the disease in the other is in a progressive condition." By October 21 of the following year, three more cases had been sent to the island, two from Vancouver and one from Victoria.[114] In his 1905 annual report Dr. Robertson said that the provincial government assumed responsibility for the lazaretto on January 1 of that year, during which time a sixth patient had been added to the colony. The D'Arcy Island lazaretto thus passed out of the interest and responsibility of the City of Victoria.

CHAPTER FOUR

Ordinary
ideas of humanity

SINCE THE FIRE of June 15, 1899, the condition of the residents had considerably deteriorated and, judging from the decrease in newspaper articles, the interest of the press (and perhaps the public) had likewise substantially diminished. Throughout this period, and extending to January 1, 1905, most of the interest in the lazaretto was focused upon efforts to persuade either the dominion or provincial governments to take over responsibility for its operations and maintenance. These efforts began shortly after the colony's establishment when it became apparent that the facility was going to be costly for the contributing cities, mainly Victoria and

Vancouver. After several months of unsuccessful negotiations in January of 1892 the dominion government granted the cities of Victoria and Vancouver a total of $1,000 as compensation for their expenses regarding D'Arcy Island.[115] Following more pleadings, in 1895 the dominion government granted an additional $1,000[116] and, in a move to get Victoria and the province off its back, amended the Quarantine Act of 1872 to exclude leprosy, thus making the lazaretto a matter of public health and the responsibility of the province.[117] In March of 1898 Ottawa sent another $947.59,[118] which is precisely the amount Victoria spent on the facility in 1897.

Ultimately, negotiations between British Columbia and Ottawa regarding disbursement of poll tax revenues began to bear fruit. In 1900 the province received 25% of the poll tax collected for the year ending in June, a sum of over $47,000. Following the increase in poll tax from $50 to $100 in 1901, it was agreed in 1902 that the province would receive half the revenue in exchange for taking over responsibility for the lazaretto. In October of 1903 the province bore the expenses incurred, but it wasn't until January 1 of 1905 that it assumed full responsibility after reimbursing the cities of Victoria, Vancouver and Nanaimo for their cumulative incurred expenses.[119]

The province having taken charge of the lazaretto, the Secretary of the Provincial Board of Health, Dr. C.J.

Fagan, wasted no time in inspecting conditions on the island, in the company of Victoria's sanitary inspector, a Mr. Wilson. Steps were taken to have supplies delivered monthly (presumably the services of Captain Johnson of Sidney were considered no longer necessary). During the summer of 1905 several discussions ensued regarding the possibility of the D'Arcy Island lepers being sent to Tracadie and, during a planned trip to Europe, Dr. Fagan made arrangements to visit that facility and also to have talks in Ottawa on this subject.

During the 18 months between the time when the provincial government assumed responsibility and when the federal government took over, little is known of the fortunes of the island's inhabitants except that as of April 1, 1907, the population of the island had increased to eight. On July 11, 1906, following passage of the Leprosy Act on June 26, the dominion government assumed full responsibility for D'Arcy Island.

Once it was in the hands of the dominion government the lazaretto became an entirely different kind of facility: one of detention and medical treatment mainly for Chinese lepers prior to their deportation back to China, and, after 1917, when deportations were disallowed, their care until they were released as cured or they died. During the summer of 1906 it became apparent that the dominion government was considering plans to move the leper colony to Albert Head near Victoria, much to the consternation of the local residents. After much furious letter-writing and telegram-sending it was decided that Albert Head would not do and that a new facility would be built on the west side of D'Arcy Island. Within a short time after assuming responsibility, Dr. A.T. Watt, Superintendent of B.C. Quarantines, informed the minister of Agriculture that a guardian and a Chinese interpreter had been placed on the island, that weekly supplies of fresh meat, fish, fruit and vegetables were being delivered and that dressings for wounds and oral doses of chaulmoogra oil were being given to the patients.[120] After 15 years of being stockpiled to die without medical treatment, these unfortunate people were finally treated as human beings.

In 1907, Dr. Watt advised Dr. F. Montizambert, Director General of Public Health in the Department of Agriculture, that the eight lepers resident on D'Arcy Island had, with some difficulty, been successfully returned to China where they each were given $300 in gold. Seven of them were placed in the care of the Presbyterian Mission to Lepers in Canton; the eighth decided to return to his family. Dr. Watt concluded, "I may say there has nothing occurred around Victoria for some time which has been the subject of such universal gratification as has been the departure of these lepers for their own country."[121] The cost of returning each man to China was $650.

Following the deportation of the first eight men, the old buildings, shacks and lean-tos of the colony were

Remains of the caretaker's cottage, constructed on the northwest shore of D'Arcy Island in 1907-1908.

burned to the ground and replaced by two small, two-room buildings constructed by the Department of Public Works on the southwest shore of nearby Little D'Arcy Island, some 400 metres from the original site on the larger island.[122] One of the rooms was intended for an interpreter. During 1907-1908 a cottage for the permanent guardian was built on D'Arcy Island's northwest shore. Dr. Montizambert, in 1916, wrote to J.B. Hunter, deputy minister of Public Works, saying, "There are two concrete double shacks at the south end of Little D'Arcy Island, for the residence of the lepers. When a residence was required for the guardian, it was placed, *without my knowledge* [author's emphasis] at the extreme northern end of the larger of the two D'Arcy Islands, about a mile away from the shacks."[123] Thus, for almost ten years, the Director General of Public Health in Ottawa, and the senior bureaucrat responsible for the D'Arcy Island(s) facility, was unaware that the caretaker lived on a different island than did his patients. Presumably Dr. Watt knew because he would have had to visit the facility on a regular basis. Insofar as the caretaker's cottage and the accommodations on Little D'Arcy Island were built under the supervision of Mr. Wilson, the caretaker and former sanitation officer, it was probably he who organized the physical separation, presumably because he did not wish to live close to the lazaretto's residents.

Dr. Montizambert's letter is of further interest because its main purpose was to request the Department of Public Works to construct another "shack" for a leper who was originally from Chile. The request was for one of two solutions: either the concrete shacks on Little D'Arcy Island be moved closer to the caretaker's house, or a new residence for the Chilean be constructed there. At this time the Little D'Arcy Island shacks were unoccupied and Dr. Montizambert felt that "the prospect of sending this sick Chilean to live by himself at the south end of the island [meaning on Little D'Arcy Island], so far away from the guardian *does not seem compatible with ordinary ideas of humanity* [author's emphasis]." There was an occasion, however, when a lone Chinese man occupied one of these shacks, but, being "only a Chinaman" he was presumably not deserving of the "ordinary ideas of humanity."

During the following year (1917) two new residences were built not far from the caretaker's cottage and the buildings on Little D'Arcy Island were abandoned. Dr. Montizambert's attitude is further illustrated in a memorandum to the minister of Agriculture on September 17, 1917: "In the first place there is the pitiable case of Mr. Davis, white Canadian, whom it is hardly seemly to turn into joint quarters with the Chinese and Chilean lepers."

In 1907-1908 three more men were returned to China, followed by another two in 1908-1909. The main difficulty in returning these people was finding a steamship that would agree to take them and prepare isolation quarters on board. Such opportunities were rare, so it was necessary to maintain the island as a holding and treatment area until vessels could be found. During 1909-1910 no new cases were brought to the island; however, a boathouse and dock for a small gasoline launch were constructed by the guardian as well as a workshop, woodshed and cellar associated with his house. During the next year a Hindu from a railway construction camp near Kamloops was held at the lazaretto for several weeks prior to his return to India. In his March 31, 1912, report Dr. Watt said that no patients had occupied the island during the previous 12 months. A year later he said four Chinese lepers were accommodated while awaiting deportation, during which time one of them died. The expenses of these deportations were met by the steamship companies, which had brought the men to Canada.

In July of 1913 Dr. Watt died and Dr. H. Rundle Nelson replaced him as Medical Superintendent of William Head Quarantine Station. In 1914, he stated that there was only one Chinese leper detained at D'Arcy Island awaiting deportation. This occurred on May 13, 1915 after which time the lazaretto was again empty throughout the remainder of the year and much of the next. As described in his 1917 report five men were detained: a Russian, two Chinese, one Japanese and a

"Chilean-Kanaka" (Kanaka referring to a native of Hawaii), this last being very difficult to handle, necessitating a separate house to be constructed for him. In the same report Dr. Nelson advised Dr. Montizambert of the death of the guardian, who was temporarily replaced by the former "night watchman," W. Young.

By March 31, 1918, H.T. McKee had been appointed guardian, and his wife, a nurse, undertook volunteer work with the patients. The work of Mrs. McKee was extremely valuable, allowing for application of other forms of treatment in addition to, or instead of, chaulmoogra oil which, when taken in oral doses large enough to do any good, resulted in pronounced nausea and discomfort. One man, whose symptoms had been substantially reduced, was released from the island but was unable to find any work, so Dr. Nelson arranged with Dr. Montizambert for him to be given a monthly pension of $20. He also arranged for bi-annual payments of $25 to be sent to resident lepers' dependants in China. In 1917 further deportations were disallowed and the remaining six years saw the population steady at between four and five patients, two being released as cured. One of these was the only woman sent to the island, a girl of 16 named Lee Noey Quong; with the financial assistance of her friends she eventually sailed for China on December 28, 1922, where she entered the leper hospital at Hong Chow. In 1920 Mrs. McKee was hired as assistant guardian and remained in that post until the facility closed in 1924.

On March 20, 1924, the remaining five residents were removed from D'Arcy Island and taken to a newly established facility on Bentinck Island, immediately west of the entrance to Pedder Bay, near the quarantine station at William Head. Thus it was that the 33-year history of the D'Arcy Island leper colony ended.

Following this closure, D'Arcy Island was the focus of interest for its potential use as a confinement centre for members of the Sons of Freedom sect of the Doukhobors. The dominion government, however, finally determined on Piers Island near Swartz Bay, close to the northern end of the Saanich Peninsula, as the location of the detention centre.

In October of 1958 the provincial government set aside D'Arcy Island for future development as a marine park, and it received its official status on January 4, 1967.

The site of the original colony as it looks today from offshore.

D'Arcy Island
June 24, 1899

Chunwan
Sun Way
China

Ah Lan,

My name is Lung Hing. I write to tell you that your husband, Lim Sam, died several days ago in a fire. Like me, he got leprosy and was put on this island many years ago. I have only been here about two years myself but in that time I got to know and like your husband. He was a good man and he often spoke about you and your son, even though he knew that he would not see you again. He never wrote to you because he felt so ashamed at being a leper and being made a prisoner. I knew his feelings because they were the same as mine.

He told me that, for some years, his closest friends were two other lepers that lived here until they died. They were Nap Sing and Sim Lee, both much older than Lim Sam. The three used to talk long into the nights, sometimes about home, sometimes about death and dying, and at other times about life here. They played cards a lot and smoked opium whenever the supply boat brought it. We all smoke opium when we can. It helps the days and the winter storms pass.

Lim Sam was never satisfied with the bare walls of his cubicle. He used to decorate it with the pages of newspapers brought from Victoria by the supply boat that comes once every three months. He tried to get Chinese papers as often as he could. Because he could read he was often asked to tell the others what was happening in the world, like the start of the Boer War in Africa. He said the English liked war and started one whenever they could. Once he got a Chinese paper that told us about Wilfrid Laurier, the new prime minister. The paper said that he was going to increase the poll tax on Chinese immigrants from $50 to $100. Lim Sam saved the paper to wipe his ass with, then he put it up on the wall— shit and all.

He told me that soon after coming here he planned to escape and somehow get back to China. He even built a small raft from driftwood and one summer night he paddled alone out into the cold water. The raft quickly came apart in the choppy water and soon he was adrift, holding onto a log and being pushed by the strong current and wind that suddenly came up. He managed to get to a nearby island where he nearly died from exposure and exhaustion. Some fishermen saw him and told the authorities. He was returned to the colony about a week later. He had lost a lot of weight and the will to try again. After that he never left the colony, even for a walk. Actually, none of us do. Most of us can't walk very far because we are weak and because, with no feeling in our feet, we could cut ourselves and easily die from blood poisoning. It's not that we're afraid to die, most of us hope for it, but to die from poisoning is very painful. For those of us who can still feel pain, we don't like it.

When the supply boat comes it always brings the Victoria sanitation officer but sometimes also Dr. Fraser. He's a good man but is unable to help the sick and dying very much. He comes mainly to inspect the buildings, to see if they are clean enough, and to see who of us is next to die. He has often said that he has been trying to get the Canadian government to take over the colony so that we could get good medical help. So far he and others have not been successful. I suspect that is because we are Chinese. The Whites hate us. If we were Whites we would be looked after in a good hospital and allowed to go home someday. But we are only Chinese. Instead we get imprisoned on a tiny island to die alone and without help.

Lim Sam would sit for hours on a big log down on the beach in front of the building. He enjoyed watching the sea gulls as they drifted overhead. On the same day as the fire he asked me to write to you after he died. He was sick and very weak, blind in one eye and with only stumps for fingers and toes. He had sores everywhere on his body. He could not write. He said to me that he wanted you to know what happened. He remembered you standing in a doorway when he left. You were waving. He liked that.

Lung Hing

Concrete foundation for a detention cottage constructed on the northwest shore of D'Arcy Island in 1917.

Piece of an iron wood-stove door found at the Darcy Island colony site.

a Look back

THE ORIGINAL SITE of the lazaretto has been a subject of some confusion and misinformation, for, strange as it may seem, there are no municipal, provincial or federal government maps showing it, nor any descriptions of its location apart from the *Daily Colonist* article of May 15, 1891, which vaguely said that it was located "at the south-east [end of the island]." As late as 1922 the dominion Departments of Health and Public Works had differing information, the former believing the original site to have been on D'Arcy Island[124] and the latter holding the view that it was on Little D'Arcy Island.[125] Even within the Department of Health confusion was evident as shown in a memo which said that the original site was on the smaller island,[126] a view recently argued by D.E. French.[127]

Arguments supporting the original site as being at the current location of the D'Arcy Island Marine Park campground are, however, conclusive. As mentioned earlier, several artefacts, including parts of beds and wood stoves, stone building-footings, several pieces of broken ceramic kitchenware and fruit trees have been found, as well as six possible graves. On (British) Admiralty Chart 2840, published in 1911 and including information compiled from British and American surveys to 1908, D'Arcy Island is identified as a "Leper St^n" and the symbols for two buildings are shown adjacent to the north shore of the bay fronting the modern campground. These two structures are seen in a photograph in the Hall and Nelson (1898) article; the easternmost is the six-cubicle building constructed by the municipal government of Victoria whereas the structure to the west is the accommodation built by Vancouver authorities a few months later. A comparison of the earlier photos shows that the shapes and detailed characteristics of the prominent rock outcrops behind the two men (photo taken in 1892?) are readily recognizable today. Moreover, the bifurcated tree behind the left (west) end of the building as seen in two of the photos taken in 1897 is still standing.

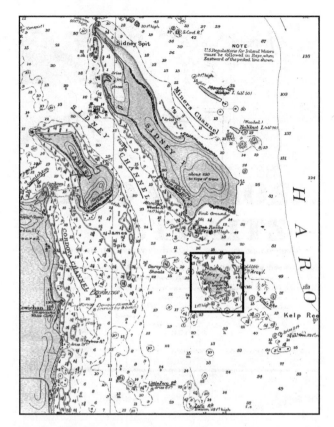

Portion of British Admiralty chart 2840, published in 1911 and compiled from British and United States government surveys to 1908. D'Arcy Island (as indicated within the black rectangle) is identified as a Leper Station. The symbols for two buildings along the north shore of the bay on the east shore are clearly visible on the original chart.

Insofar as the campground was built as recently as 1997, it is not surprising that visitors to the site have not yet disturbed the artefacts, nor would many know that it was the site of a leper colony at which 15 men died a century earlier. Personnel of the B.C. Provincial Parks Branch were unaware that they had constructed a campground on the original site of the lazaretto. In October of 1999 B.C. Parks let a contract to I.R. Wilson Consultants Ltd. for an archaeological assessment of the area within and adjacent to the campground. This investigation confirmed that the campground was indeed constructed on the original site of the lazaretto.[128] Ten cairns of rock were found which were probably made by the residents; without further study and excavation it cannot be said that all or any of these cairns are graves.

The character of the beach in the bay may have been a significant factor in the choice of this site for the lazaretto. Whereas other shorelines on the island are either rocky or composed of angular, coarse rock fragments, unsuitable for beaching wooden boats except during the calmest of seas, the beach below the lazaretto, as shown in some of the photos, consists of a thick mantle of rounded pebbles forming a berm, seaward of which the bottom quickly deepens. At moderate tide and gentle wind this would have allowed the small supply steamers to tie to the beach, bow-on into the gravel, with a stern anchor deployed in deep water. Supplies could be easily off-loaded, as could visiting authorities. Although southeasterly winds are common, particularly during the winter, the effects of surf upon the beach are reduced due to partial protection provided by the small peninsula at the southeast end of the island as well as by Unit Rocks and Little D'Arcy Island. Thus the small vessels were moderately safe from surf damage. In the event of stronger blows, the vessels could anchor offshore where a sand-and-mud bottom provides fair holding ground.

Not all was well with the site of the colony. During the winter strong to gale-force southeast winds are common. The location of the building was about 100 metres above and parallel to the beach. During winter storms, with winds frequently exceeding 50 knots across an unobstructed fetch of several kilometres, the structure would have had to withstand considerable force and any necessary outdoor activities by the residents would have been very difficult and uncomfortable. Moreover, the frequency of these storms would have been such as to cause considerable prudence among the authorities in scheduling supply runs. To be caught at sea in a small steamer in such conditions would have been very hazardous, as there was nowhere that the vessel could go for protection. As described in the endnotes, Sanitation Officer Chipchase was thrown overboard in rough sea conditions during a supply run.

The character of the gravel berm is interesting insofar as it has remained unchanged for at least over 100 years. The size range of the pebbles and their roundness

The bifurcated tree
(still alive) shown in
earlier photos.

indicates that the beach has remained in dynamic equilibrium with dominantly northwesterly driven wave systems for a long time. Their uniform composition, consisting of locally derived Palaeozoic volcanic rocks, and the high degree of size sorting, indicates that little material is annually added to or subtracted from the beach.

Throughout its earliest 15 years, between 1891 and 1906, the lazaretto on D'Arcy Island lay in quiet and ignorant isolation from many of the events that ultimately shaped the twentieth century and the future of humankind. It was a time of widespread imperialism and its associated wars: the Sino-Japanese War (1895), the Spanish-American War (1898), the Boxer Rebellion (1900), the Boer War (1899-1902), the Russo-Japanese War (1904-1905) and many others. In 1903 the Ford Motor Company was formed and in December of that year Orville Wright kept a man-made machine aloft for 12 seconds above a field at Kitty Hawk, North Carolina. In September of the founding year of the lazaretto Herman Melville died, Adolf Hitler was 17 months old, and nearly ten years later Queen Victoria's death ushered in the Edwardian Era. In 1901 the world learned that Pablo Picasso had painted his *Blue Room* in Paris, just after Ernest Hemingway was born. In that same year Guglielmo Marchese Marconi successfully transmitted radio signals across the Atlantic from Poldhu in Cornwall, England, to St. John's, Newfoundland. In

1903 Pierre and Marie Curie shared the Nobel Prize in physics with Antoine Henri Becquerel for their discoveries of radioactivity and two years later Albert Einstein published a paper entitled *On the Electrodynamics of Moving Bodies* which became known as his Special Theory of Relativity. On April 18, 1906, three months before the dominion government assumed responsibility for the lazaretto, the downtown area of San Francisco and much of its residential area were destroyed by fire caused by an earthquake along the infamous San Andreas Fault.

In Canada, the year 1891 saw the death of Sir John A. Macdonald and the appearance of the "Great White Empresses," the *Empress of India, Empress of Japan* and *Empress of China,* all built by the C.P.R. to enhance Canadian trade with the Far East and, incidentally, to bring more and more cheap Oriental labour to British Columbia. Sir Wilfrid Laurier led the Liberal Party to victory in 1896 and ultimately, but reluctantly, acceding to British Columbia's demands, increased the poll tax on Chinese immigrants in 1901, and again, in 1903. In 1905 Alberta and Saskatchewan were made provinces. Throughout this period anti-Oriental sentiment in British Columbia remained high; many anti-Oriental bills passed in the provincial legislature were disallowed by the dominion government which wanted to retain good trading relations with Japan whose immigrants were commonly included in the bills. These rejections

View westward along the pebble beach berm fronting the original site of the lazaretto.

of provincial legislation caused much resentment throughout British Columbia, feelings, which were not greatly different from those felt in some quarters today.

There are a great many aspects of the history of the D'Arcy Island colony which deserve comment. One of the most troublesome centres on Victoria City Council's refusal to provide proper medical care for the forcibly interned residents. Since the council had taken the action to establish the lazaretto in the first place, one would think it a logical necessity for a medically trained guardian to be housed on the island and supplied with medicines for the residents. Obviously the city council didn't think so. To them it was enough to provide the basic necessities of life. Their mission was to rid the city of lepers, not to establish a facility for their medical care. For that they hoped to intimidate the dominion government into taking them off the hook. In truth, however, they had no basis for assuming that would happen and they were told very early on that Ottawa would not comply. They knew of course that it would be extremely costly to provide proper care and also that it would be very difficult to find someone with the proper qualifications to live in isolation on the island among people with such a dreaded disease. Nevertheless, having chosen this course, it can be argued that the city council should have at least tried. They probably didn't because the lepers were "just Chinamen." Had they been Caucasian it is certain that adequate medical treatment would have been made available as it was at the lazaretto at Tracadie, New Brunswick.

Although the dominion government refused to accept responsibility for D'Arcy Island, it could have agreed to the suggestion of Dr. A.C. Smith, the medical director at Tracadie, that the lepers of British Columbia be sent to the leper hospital in New Brunswick where they too would have received proper medical care at a much lower cost than on D'Arcy Island; his letter in this regard to W.B. Scarth, deputy minister of Agriculture in Ottawa, was ignored.[129]

The provincial government was also culpable; their Board of Health and the attorneys general were well aware of the situation on the island and yet they did nothing to relieve medical suffering during the 15 years the province argued with Ottawa over responsibility. The fact that the dominion government established a program of supervised medical care *immediately* upon assuming responsibility for the facility lends strong support to the notion that the City of Victoria and the provincial government owe an apology to the memory of the men who suffered miserably and died from medical neglect while under their care.

By what authority did the City of Victoria apprehend and forcibly confine lepers to D'Arcy Island? Although the city fathers realized that they had no authority to expend public funds on the lazaretto,[130] they nonetheless probably assumed that their Consolidated Health Bylaw of 1886 gave them the legal basis to act as they did. Also, in 1892 the provincial government passed legislation which could have retroactively allowed the municipality to establish and operate the lazaretto should anyone have chosen to challenge the Corporation of Victoria.[131] Section 106 of the provincial Municipal Act, 1892, gave municipalities the right to spend revenues for establishing and maintaining institutions for the support of people with contagious or infectious diseases. Moreover, the city's Health Bylaw of 1893, which replaced the earlier 1886 bylaw, allowed for the medical health officer to apprehend and isolate people with infectious diseases. At the time Canada had no national health act, thus these local bylaws existed in a vacuum, possibly without legal authority. It wasn't until June of 1906, when the dominion government promulgated the Leprosy Act, that persons with Hansen's disease could be forcibly confined without fear of legitimate legal argument to the contrary. [132]

Once on the island the residents depended for their lives on the assumed certainty and regularity of the quarterly supply visits which, throughout the period when the City of Victoria was solely responsible for maintenance of the colony, were carried out with almost religious zeal. The long-standing commitment to these visits was probably, in part, conscience driven. Although civic administrations changed during this period, incoming councils knew that people were being placed on the island to die without medical support. And although they were considered to be "just Chinamen" the authorities may have felt compelled, out of conscience, to give whatever assistance they could to these dying men. Anything they asked for was provided, including opium which, to some extent, may have relieved their suffering.

The activities of medical personnel during the quarterly supply visits are difficult to assess, even when the doctors were accompanied by a reporter who wrote a resulting article. With but one exception, and that late in the lazaretto's history, no descriptions of medical ministry are given, either in annual reports or by the press. What did these doctors actually do when they made a visit? With the lepers' badly ulcerated limbs and other traumas, the need for bandaging, ointment applications and other types of medical attention would have been obvious, particularly as the visits were three months apart. Yet there is no mention of any such treatment. Were the doctors' interests simply limited to noting the degree of advancement of the disease so that in their annual reports to city council they could allude to actual as well as anticipated deaths? After a period of three months, every patient would have needed attention, which would have taken a considerable amount of time, perhaps a few hours. And yet, according to several *Daily Colonist* articles, the total round trips of the *Sadie* show that the time actually spent on the island was often less than an hour. Despite the lack of information on this subject it is likely that the doctors visited the island with their ever-present little black bags; it is difficult to believe that these remained closed throughout their visits.

Since there was widespread misapprehension that the disease was dangerously contagious, did visiting medical and sanitary officers, as well as tourist dignitaries, take any precautionary steps to prevent their being infected? In none of the visits to the colony by officials that included the press is there any indication such steps were taken. The photographs do not show that they were wearing protective clothing or any other paraphernalia associated with disease control. It is known, however, that at least initially, the crews of the steamers would not carry the quarterly supplies ashore unless the residents were on the veranda of their house. This comparatively casual attitude on the part of Victoria's medical and sanitary officials is in marked contrast to that adopted of Vancouver physicians.

As late as September of 1904, the Vancouver *Daily Province* reported upon the delivery of a Chinese leper to D'Arcy Island; he was wrapped in blankets and confined to the stern of the steamer "so that he will not be near anyone on the trip." The Vancouver medical health officer, a Dr. Underhill, was to "take a rubber cloak of some sort in which to perform the inspection, and will then leave this and his other clothing behind at the island, in order that he may run no danger of bringing the contagion away with him." The residents must have been amused as they watched the good doctor strip himself naked and climb aboard the steamer where he took an antiseptic bath.[133]

During the first 15 years of the lazaretto's existence there was a widespread lack of common understanding about Hansen's disease throughout the medical profession. Influential medical men such as Sir William Osler and Dr. F. Montizambert held completely different views about leprosy's dangers, views of which both were undoubtedly well aware. Although it is tempting to seek and cast blame in situations such as this, it is the nature of science that is at fault, and not necessarily its practitioners. By its very nature, science is, and must be, a conservative discipline. It depends upon experimentation, observation, hypothesis and proof, each of which, in most cases, requires years of effort. And even when all that is in place, there are those who cling to old ideas because they have always worked, or because the individuals are spectators, not innovators. Ideas concerning the danger of leprosy were in a state of change when the City Council of Victoria established the D'Arcy Island colony. In many instances the press referred to its degree of contagiousness as "problematical." Moreover, at the time of the problems with the Vancouver lepers, the Vancouver *Daily World* published an interview with a Mrs. J.B. Ker, who held contrary views on its dangers based upon her extensive experience with the disease in Norway where the disease was considered to be non-contagious.[134] It seems, however, that the public's fear of the disease prevented rapid acceptance of alternative information, even within large segments of the medical profession; it took several decades for medical, public and political attitudes to change. The slow pace of that change as it was applied to the D'Arcy Island leper colony had little to do with anti-Chinese prejudice, despite the assertions of some to the contrary.

Another area where medical information is lacking is in descriptions of the initial conditions of the residents, their deterioration through time and what killed them. The only details of any kind were provided by *Daily*

Colonist articles following visits by the press, and the few photographs. Of all those who died, it is known that one died from tuberculosis, one by fire and one was possibly murdered. Another was described as having lost his voice and was not expected to live long; he probably died of suffocation.[135] With no death records, coroners' records or medical records the fate of any of the others will never be known; however, that they died without medical care is certain. Due to their weakened condition, their immune systems were probably significantly degraded, and what killed them was toxicity set up by infections of various kinds and, because of the wet and cool winter climate, one or more of the various types of pneumonia. Their isolation would have prevented most communicable diseases from affecting them, except perhaps those which they may have brought with them, in which case several deaths would have occurred quickly; for this there is no evidence.

Living in isolation and without medical resources to relieve day-to-day infirmities, the residents may have exploited any natural remedies available to them. Although it is unlikely that many, if any, fully explored their tiny island, it is probable that they took some advantage of the many plants that grew within a short distance of their colony: wild ginger and onion, for example, in combination being a well-known remedy for colds. Also, if they possessed specialized knowledge they might have concocted various teas from plants for the relief of aches and pains, fevers, stomach ailments and headaches. For the more serious diseases such as pneumonia, all they could do would be to keep their companions warm, to help them to the latrine pit or empty a bedside bucket and to feed them as best they could. In regard to sanitary conditions, the sanitary officers probably arranged for or oversaw the placement and digging of latrine pits and the abandonment of old ones, although, not surprisingly, no mention is made of this necessary activity in any of the contemporary press articles, catering as they did to Victorian and/or Edwardian sensitivities.

Another subject on which little information is available is water supply, for personal use as well as for the large garden. Only two contemporary documents refer to the subject: a May 15, 1891, *Daily Colonist* article claiming that the lazaretto would be located within 100 feet of fresh water, and a letter, written in 1906 by Dr. A.T. Watt, Superintendent of B.C. Quarantines, saying that the residents had to haul water a distance of 300 yards.[136] According to a recent Victoria *Times Colonist* article "the only fresh water came from an abandoned well";[137] there is no evidence of a well. The nearest source of fresh water was a northeasterly trending, broad, boggy area supporting abundant deciduous trees and bog plants and located about 75 metres northwest of the building site. In early September of 1999, fresh water was found beneath about six inches of humus that filled a depression at the edge of

Bog area north of the buildings, from which the residents obtained their drinking and garden water.

the bog. Given that this is the driest time of the year, when water tables substantially subside due to lack of recharge, it is likely that the boggy area in general and the depression in particular could have provided sufficient water for personal and garden use during the late fall, winter and spring when the water table returned to normal levels. Department of Environment records show that during the period that the colony occupied this site, the annual amounts of rainfall were much as they are today and that periods of drought commonly occurred during July and August with heavy rains returning in November.[138] It is also probable that throughout the year rain water was collected in rain barrels located below the eaves of the building.

It is doubtful that the supply of water was always sufficient for the needs of the colony. In his letter cited above, Watt also said that, "... there is consequently not the amount used which cleanliness requires." During the peak summer drought both the paucity of water in the depression and the physical difficulty the residents would have had collecting adequate quantities would have meant the supply was less than adequate for their personal needs, let alone the garden. Moreover, the rain barrels (if any) would have been empty and it is most unlikely that useful quantities of water could have been brought on the quarterly supply runs. Thus it seems likely that during the summer months some, if not all, of the residents, suffered some degree of dehydration. As to the quality of the water, because the primary aquifer was fractured bedrock of volcanic origin, the amount of dissolved iron and magnesium would have been high, as would suspended organic matter derived from the bog plants. The water would thus have been somewhat discoloured, but otherwise drinkable.

The large vegetable garden appears to have been above the beach to the west and southwest of the two buildings and may have extended inland close to the edge of the bog. Evidence for this is provided by a broad area of young trees, probably less than 50 to 60 years old, with older, larger trees roughly defining the perimeter. This presumed garden area is flat and covered by dense salal. It is possible that a ditch system leading from the bog could have provided irrigation for the garden.

Apart from spring planting and fall harvesting of their garden, and the need to collect firewood and organize supplies, nothing is known of the daily activities of the residents. Due to their considerable disabilities and weakened condition it is doubtful that they saw more of their tiny island than the immediate surroundings of the colony. As suggested above they may have collected plants for medicinal purposes as well as harvested clams and mussels from the shoreline of their tiny bay. Some may have even fished from shore. Gambling may have occupied part of their time, as well as smoking opium whenever it was available, either from the authorities or through trading food supplies with passing fishermen. It is known that Victoria's citizenry occasionally provided supplies[139] which may have included reading materials, such as books and newspapers, for those who could read, either in Chinese or English. Mail from home? Not likely. Throughout the long, cold, wet winters, most of their time would have been spent keeping warm and just trying to endure being alive.

What was the attitude of the colony's residents toward their infirmity and their imprisonment on the island? Ng Chung tried to slit his own throat and another victim took poison rather than be sent to the lazaretto. Others tried to convince the authorities their symptoms were those of syphilis or other ailments, and not leprosy. When visited by the press none would admit to having leprosy, yet each insisted that his companions did, and they were very reluctant to have their photographs taken. All of this suggests that the residents felt profound shame for their condition, a stigma that was tens of centuries old; immutable. Their isolation from friends and relatives in Victoria and in China would surely have caused most to become extremely depressed, at least initially, for which there is abundant evidence in the reports of the *Daily Colonist.*[140] Although removed from the rising tide of anti-Orientalism in British Columbia, they nevertheless probably knew of it and felt caged and defenceless, like despised and feared animals. And yet, if the press reports are to be believed, the "unfortunates," as most called them, were glad to receive visitors, particularly on quarterly supply deliveries.

Their lot was not entirely an unhappy one for what would have befallen them had they not been taken to the island? In 1893 a significant economic depression struck western North America, and Vancouver, in particular, had very high unemployment. What were the chances of a leprous Chinese surviving at all? What were the chances that his countrymen would continue to house, feed and hide him from the authorities? The previous year a smallpox epidemic had spread throughout the Chinese population; in Victoria there were 47 cases reported and four deaths and in Vancouver several deaths occurred. Had these people remained in the cities, they would quite possibly have died of smallpox. Once the authorities in Victoria decided to construct the lazaretto, they were bound to maintain it and see to the housing, feeding and clothing of its inhabitants. Once the victims were on the island they no longer had to scrounge for food, clothing, shelter or money.

When they died, what was done with their bodies? There are no references to body disposal in any of the annual reports submitted to city council by either the medical health officers or the sanitary officers, nor are there descriptions of burials or burial sites in contemporary newspaper articles. Assuming that some of these mounds are indeed graves (awaiting confirmation by archaeological study), why do they occur in two distinct groups: one very close to the building site and the other in the forest to the northwest? The Chinese culture has a tradition of ghosts associated with the dead, thus explaining the considerable distances separating the buildings from most of the mounds in the woods. However, the two mounds close by the building site would cast doubt upon that explanation were it not for times when the surviving residents were perhaps so weak and sick that they could drag their dead companions only as far as the foot of the veranda, lay them on the ground and cover them as best they could. It is also possible that the mounds close to the building mark former garbage sites.

Possible grave located close to the original building.

Probable grave located in the woods behind (north of) the original building.

How were these people able to function at all? Without fingers, or any sensation whatever in their hands and feet, how did they handle a rake, a shovel or a frying pan? How did they haul buckets of water 250 feet from the bog to the building? They wouldn't have known where their feet were without looking. Without the sensation of pain, they must have burnt and cut themselves often. Rats may have eaten their fingers while they slept. Unnoticed pebbles and sharp objects in their shoes would have cut their feet. Perhaps their feet were so ulcerated and the flesh so destroyed that some walked on bare bone. Some had lost their sight. Their faces commonly were a swollen hideousness, oozing tubercles everywhere, eyebrows gone, nose collapsed, lips bloated and senseless— no wonder they didn't want their pictures taken. That these people were able to function at all, let alone carve a garden out of the forest, plant it, maintain it and keep themselves as a functioning, co-operative, micro-civilization is a profound testament to the power of the human spirit.

How was it that an isolated group of doomed aliens from a different culture was able to organize and conduct itself in such a manner, particularly when the composition of the group was constantly changing? Under ordinary circumstances it might be expected that without strong leadership and a legal structure imposing limits on behaviour, a society would rapidly decay, and self-discipline would weaken, leading to chaos, filth and other forms of social corruption. Sir William Golding's *Lord of the Flies* comes to mind. Although there were variations in the composition of their society and changes in personalities, it seems that the residents of D'Arcy Island were able to create an environment based upon inter-personal respect and mutual tolerance. The quarterly visits by the sanitary and medical health officers would have encouraged the residents to maintain a certain level of civilized behaviour, but they would not have been enough to regulate the society as much as it seems to have regulated itself. Food and other supplies must have been divided, either formally or informally, to allow each resident fair and adequate access. "To each according to his needs." Likewise, the various daily chores such as firewood collecting, gardening and garbage disposal must have been carried out in accordance with the other half of Marx's famous dictum: "from each according to his ability." But how? It appears likely that part of the answer may lie in the strong Chinese belief that the welfare of the group as a whole is more important than that of the individual. Over thousands of years the many different physical, political and economic environments of China, some in complete isolation from others, encouraged the development of mechanisms for group survival and the subjugation of individual needs. Just as the Chinese community of Victoria for its own protection probably isolated the original five lepers from the majority of their society, so perhaps did the lepers of

D'Arcy Island, employing this same principle, establish an internal organization designed to encourage group co-operation and prevent social breakdown and chaos at the expense of individual needs. Unfortunately there are no documents which can shed light on the structure and processes of this organization, or even attest to its existence.

To what extent did racist attitudes affect the residents of D'Arcy Island? Although anti-Chinese prejudice had much to do with the manner in which the residents were treated, an interesting inverse relationship between prejudice and politics developed, resulting in benefit to the island community. For many years the dominion government disallowed provincial anti-Oriental legislation because it wanted to maintain good relationships with China and Japan, yet at the same time it collected a head tax on each Chinese immigrant to British Columbia. The province turned this against the senior government by claiming that insofar as it was the latter which disallowed such legislation and who permitted immigration in the first place, it should return 50% of the head tax to the province for application toward the expenses of the lazaretto. Against this argument the dominion government had no legitimate defence and it was finally forced to assume responsibility for the colony through promulgation of the Leprosy Act. So it could be argued that in this way, anti-Chinese prejudice actually helped the residents of D'Arcy Island to ultimately get proper medical care and more humane treatment.

And finally, for the sake of contrast, the following is a short history and description of operations at the lazaretto at Tracadie, New Brunswick.[141] Leprosy first appeared in the Maritimes in the early 1840s when several French-speaking Acadians contracted the disease. A facility to contain them was built on Sheldrake Island in the Gulf of St. Lawrence in 1844 which, five years later, was moved to nearby Tracadie on the northeast coast of New Brunswick. The lazaretto was primarily a hospital within which patients were fed, clothed, housed and medically treated. Until 1880, the facility was operated by the New Brunswick government through its Board of Health whose members appeared to be more interested in serving themselves through lucrative contracts than in aiding the residents. Although political infighting as well as other failings of government affected it, the facility at Tracadie was served throughout its history by dedicated medical and religious men and, after 1868, by several Sisters of Les Hospitalières de Saint-Joseph of Montreal. For the most part the residents were not forcibly confined nor prevented from access to the town. Their spiritual needs were met by the town's church and access to family members was permitted. In November of 1880 the lazaretto came under the jurisdiction of the dominion Department of Agriculture which continued to employ the Sisters for its management and operations. The lazaretto closed its doors in 1965. Tracadie was an institution run and managed by caring people for the benefit of the residents. On the other hand, D'Arcy Island was more akin to hell on earth.

For 15 years there existed, on D'Arcy Island, a society of outcasts. It was a society of people who, through no fault of their own, were the victims of disease, medical and social ignorance, racial prejudice and political neglect at all levels. They had come from China looking for a better life and found only suffering and death. No one holds them in memory. They died unquoted and unrecorded. That they lived is acknowledged only by 15 unmarked graves on a tiny island in Haro Strait. May this book return a measure of value to their lives.

Epilogue

SINCE THIS BOOK was completed the Parks Branch of the B.C. Ministry of Environment, Lands and Parks, at its campsite on D'Arcy Island's east shore, has established a pictorial display outlining the history of the lazaretto. Also, at the same location, the Corporation of the City of Victoria has placed a bronze memorial to the men who died on the island between the years 1891 and 1906. A sense of closure has finally been rendered to this sad story.

Endnotes

1. The term derives from the parable of the rich man and Lazarus in the *New Testament* (Luke 16). It is synonymous with leprosarium.
2. It is the Chinese custom to give the surname first followed by the given name(s). The name "Ah" was commonly appended to the given name as a salutation by a close friend or relative.
3. Dr. Paul Brand provided many useful comments following his review of an earlydraft of this chapter; his comments are herein included.
4. In fairness to the "people of *Leviticus*" it should be said that it was written for a tribe of nomads, living in tents, and travelling in a great crowd. How do you enforce isolation in such a situation except to declare that victims of contagious diseases must remain "outside the camp?" Dr. Paul Brand, personal communication, November 2, 1999.
5. C. Everett Koop, United States Surgeon General from 1981 to 1989.
6. The 15th International Congress on Leprosy—Beijing, September 1998.
7. Morton, James, 1974.
8. Ballantyne, J.W., ed., 1912, p.390.
9. Victoria *Daily Times*, October 11, 1906.
10. Dr. Paul Brand, personal communication, 1999.
11. Foster, F.P., 1897.
12. Gussow, Z., 1989.
13. The provincial government managed the facility between January 1895 and June 1906.
14. Victoria City Council Minutes, March 4, 1891.
15. Akrigg, G.P.V. and Akrigg, H.B., 1988.
16. Muller, J.E., 1980.
17. Thomson, R.E., 1981.
18. Known locally at the time as Holland Bay, after the Victoria alderman who had the most to do with establishing the lazaretto.
19. *Daily Colonist*, May 15, 1891.
20. Some information was obtained from annual reports submitted at the close of fiscal years beginning on April 1 of one year and ending March 31 of the following year.

21. Letter from Quarantine Officer at William Head Quarantine Station to Dr. D.A. Clark, Assistant Deputy Minister of Health, Ottawa, July 17, 1922. Also, letter from Dr. F. Montizambert, Director General of Public Health to J.B. Hunter, Esq., Deputy Minister of Public Works, Ottawa, October 17, 1916.

22. French, D.E., 1995 a,b.

23. Lai, David, 1991.

24. Morton, James, 1974.

25. Ships' passenger lists for the 1890s show that about one out of every three Chinese immigrants chose "laundryman" as his registration profession.

26. E.B. Wickberg in Hurtig, 1988, p.416.

27. *Ibid.*

28. Morton, James, 1974.

29. Anti-Chinese prejudice in Nanaimo was also very strong where the Chinese worked as cheap labour in the coal mines.

30. *Daily Colonist*, November 17, 1891.

31. *Daily Colonist*, May 22, 1891. This may have been Kwong Lee & Co. although it had gone bankrupt in 1885 (see Lai, 1991, p. 19, Fig. 10, and Morton, 1974, p.133).

32. French, D.E., 1995 b.

33. The term "Celestials" was commonly used at that time to refer to people from China, the Celestial Empire which is a translation of *Tien Chao,* meaning Heavenly Dynasty.

34. Sanitary Committee Report to Victoria City Council, April 22, 1891.

35. British Columbia Lands and Works Department. British Columbia Archives, C/C/30.7/G19.

36. By Executive Order in Council issued on May 13, 1891, the island was officially set aside for the city's use (*B.C. Gazette*, May 14, 1891; vol. 31, no. 19, p. 322).

37. *Daily Colonist*, May 2, 1891.

38. *Daily Colonist*, May 19, 1891.

39. There is a good possibility that Nap Sing's full name was Lam Nap Sing or Nap Lam Sing. This is suggested in a *Daily Times* news item which appeared on October 24, 1891, and quoted a message to one Yip Wing of Victoria requesting replenishment of food supplies which had run out on the island. The letter was signed by Ng Chung and Lam Ah S%. Of the original five the only one with a given name beginning with S was Nap Sing. The "%" following the S may have been employed by a *Daily Times* typesetter who was unable to read the translation of the signature of the original letter, undoubtedly in Chinese, into English. It is also possible that the *Daily Colonist* reporter, when asking his name, mistook "Lam" for "Nap" as his family name. An interesting feature of the letter was that beside the two names was written "of the place with no name." It seems that the

authorities neglected to tell them the name of the island to which they were being sent to die.

40. *Daily Colonist*, May 21, 1891.
41. *Ibid.*
42. *Daily Colonist*, February 15, 1893.
43. *Daily Colonist*, August 21, 1892.
44. *Daily Colonist*, November 15, 1891.
45. Vancouver *Daily News-Advertiser*, November 15, 1891.
46. *Daily Colonist*, August 23, 1892.
47. *Daily Times*, November 19, 1891.
48. Report of A.T. Watt, Superintendent of B.C. Quarantines to the Minister of Agriculture, Ottawa. May 31, 1913. National Archives.
49. *Daily Times*, August 23, 1892.
50. Vancouver *Daily World*, February 29, 1892.
51. *Daily Colonist*, June 16, 1895.
52. Vancouver *Daily News-Advertiser*, November 18, 1891.
53. Department of Agriculture document stamped December 31, 1896. National Archives.
54. Annual Report of Dr. G.L. Milne, Medical Health Officer, to Victoria City Council, January 1, 1893.
55. Hall, Ernest and Nelson, John, 1898.
56. Annual Reports of the Victoria City Treasurer, and *Daily Colonist*, April 22, 1903.
57. File of the Department of Agriculture, stamped May 6, 1899. No. 143391/2.
58. There is a suggestion that Sanitary Officer Bailey took a somewhat authoritarian attitude toward the lazaretto as indicated on at least two occasions when the press, presumably in jest, referred to him as "Governor-General Bailey" (*Daily Times*, Oct. 27, 1891 and *Daily Colonist*, Feb. 6, 1892).
59. *Daily Colonist*, February 7, 1892.
60. *Ibid.*
61. *Daily Colonist*, February 14, 1893.
62. The *Daily Colonist* of March 19 1893, gives his first name as Alexander, and the *Daily Colonist* of March 21 referred to him as Charles.
63. *Daily Colonist* reports of March 18 and August 2, 1893, the latter of which gives Fort Simpson which probably should read Port Simpson. A *Daily Colonist* article of January 15, 1905, refers to a Finnish settler from Malcolm Island as one of *two* white residents of the island. This conceivably could be Alexander Sundy. The other, an Irishman from the Skeena River, is doubtless imaginary.
64. Hall, Ernest and Nelson, John, 1898.
65. Unidentified National Archives document, dated May 2, 1895.

66. British Columbia Archives, Attorney General's Correspondence, 1872 - 1937. Call No. GR-0429.
67. *Ibid.*
68. *Ibid.*
69. *Daily Colonist*, August 17, 1894.
70. Department of Health memorandum, June 27, 1922.
71. Tomlinson, Alice, 1979.
72. It is probable that this was not always the case, given the advancing degrees of infirmity of the residents and thus their inability to maintain order and sanitary conditions. A case in point is given by Dr. R. L. Fraser, a later medical health officer who said in his annual report to city council on December 23, 1899, "The lazaretto is now in a truly deplorable condition. Only one man is comfortably able to work. Two of them are quite helpless, and depend for food, fire, nursing and attendance on the feeble efforts of the others."
73. *Daily Colonist*, May 12, 1894.
74. *Daily Colonist,* June 16, 1895.
75. *Daily Colonist,* May 21, 1891.
76. *Daily Colonist*, June 24, 1899.
77. *Daily Colonist*, June 16, 1895.
78. In a letter dated February 10, 1900, to a Dr. Duncan Bulkley of New York, Dr. F. Montizambert, Director General of Public Health in Ottawa inquires about the use and success of chaulmoogra oil mixed with quinine in a proportion different from that used by Dr. A.C. Smith at Tracadie, New Brunswick. (National Archives, RG 17, T-1438).
79. *Daily Colonist*, November 18, 1895.
80. Following Benjamin Bailey's retirement there were at least three sanitary officers who, at various times, administered the lazaretto. These were M.J. Conlin, ? Murray and R. Chipchase, the last of whom was out of commission following an accident in January 1894 when, on a supply run to the island in very rough seas he was swept overboard and nearly lost. It took him two and a half years before he ventured out to the island again.
81. *Daily Colonist,* February 23, 1897.
82. edical Health Officer's Report to Victoria City Council, December 1897.
83. Hall, Earnest and Nelson, John, 1898.
84. *Ibid.*
85. *Ibid.*
86. *Ibid.*
87. *Ibid.*
88. Department of Agriculture document, stamped May 8, 1898. National Archives 143391/2.

89. Letter to Hon. Senator Templeman from R.L. Fraser, April 7, 1898. National Archives.

90. *Daily Colonist,* May 5, 1898.

91. Medical Health Officer's Report to Victoria City Council, December 31, 1898.

92. Victoria City Council Minutes, December 27, 1897.

93. *Daily Colonist,* June 24, 1899.

94. Medical Health Officer's Report to Victoria City Council, December 23, 1899.

95. Tomlinson, Alice, 1979.

96. D'Arcy Island, 1891 – 1907, 1985. *British Columbia Historical News,* vol. 18, No. 3, p. 7-10.

97. What medical attention this man received is unknown.

98. *Daily Colonist,* June 24, 1899.

99. Gary Myers, Superintendent of Climate Services, Pacific and Yukon Region, Environment Canada, personal communication.

100. Insofar as the lazaretto is not visible from Cordova Bay, it is unlikely that the residents of Cordova Bay saw anything more than a distant red glow in the night sky.

101. This report is either missing from or misfiled in the records of the City of Victoria Archives. However, in his annual report of December 23, 1899, Dr. Fraser wrote: "On the night of June 15, by the extension of a bush fire, the east wing of the building occupied by the lepers was burned completely."

102. Tomlinson, Alice, 1979.

103. It is unknown whether Lim Sam's body was found inside or outside the building.

104. Victoria City Council Minutes, June 26, 1899. Discussion of a report by Dr. R.L. Fraser and W.W. Northcott. The actual report is either misfiled or missing from the City of Victoria Archives.

105. *Daily Colonist,* August 6, 1899.

106. *Daily Colonist,* June 1, 1899.

107. *Daily Colonist,* December 29, 1899.

108. *Daily Colonist,* January 18, 1890.

109. *Daily Colonist,* May 29, 1901.

110. *Daily Colonist,* May 31, 1902.

111. This is the first description of medical attention given in any reports about D'Arcy Island.

112. Joss—a Chinese god (Pidjin English derived from the Portuguese *deos*—God).

113. *Daily Colonist,* February 21, 1903.

114. Medical Health Officer's Report to Victoria City Council, December 31, 1904.

115. Annual Report of the Victoria City Treasurer, 1893.

116. *Daily Colonist,* June 26, 1895.

117. Salazar Gourley, 1985.

118. *Ibid.*
119. On March 26, 1904, the *Daily Colonist* reprinted an unusually sympathetic article from the Vancouver *Province* which argued that the lepers should be placed under dominion care at the William Head Quarantine Station.
120. Report of Dr. A.T. Watt, Superintendent of B.C. Quarantines to the Minister of Agriculture, Ottawa, April 1, 1907. British Columbia Archives, Call No. GR-2005.
121. Letter of Dr. A.T. Watt, Superintendent of B.C. Quarantines to Dr. F. Montizambert, Director General of Public Health, Ottawa, May 20, 1907. National Archives.
122. Letter from Dr. F. Montizambert, Director General of Public Health, Ottawa, to Mr. J.B. Hunter, Esq., Deputy Minister of Public Works, Ottawa, October 17, 1916.
123. *Ibid.*
124. Letter of Dr. H. Rundle Nelson, Medical Superintendent of William Head Quarantine Station, to Dr. D.A. Clark, Assistant Deputy Minister of Health, Ottawa, July 17, 1922.
125. Letter of Wm. Henderson, Resident Architect, Victoria District Resident Architect's Office, to R.C. Wright, Chief Architect, Department of Public Works, Ottawa, October 20, 1922.
126. Memorandum by "GHP," Department of Health, June 27, 1922.
127. French, D.E., 1995 a,b.
128. Hewer, Tony, 2000.
129. Letter from Dr. A.C. Smith, Tracadie, New Brunswick, to W.B. Scarth, Ottawa, April 6, 1896. National Archives.
130. Letter from H.A. Munn to T. Earl, MP, June 11, 1891.
131. Ford, Laura, 1990, p. 65-77.
132. Leprosy Act, 1906. S.C., c. 24, p. 135-139.
133. Vancouver *Daily Province*, September 26 and 28, 1904.
134. Vancouver *Daily World,* November 7, 1891.
135. *Daily Colonist*, May 29, 1901.
136. Letter of Dr. A.T. Watt, Superintendent of B.C. Quarantines to Dr. F. Montizambert, Director General of Public Health, Ottawa, May 28, 1906.
137. Victoria *Times Colonist*, October 10, 1993.
138. Canadian Climate Data for Esquimalt (1891 to 1898) and Victoria (1898 to 1906), Department of Environment.
139. *Daily Colonist*, November 2, 1893.
140. *Daily Colonist,* June 16, 1895.
141. Losier, M.J. and Pinet, C., 1984.

Bibliography

Books and Periodicals

Acs, Carolyn. 1993. "Peaceful D'Arcy Island holds grim secret." Victoria *Times Colonist*, October 10.

Akrigg, G.P.V. and Akrigg, Helen B. 1988. *British Columbia Place Names*. Sono Nis Press, Victoria.

Ballantyne, J.W., ed. 1912. *Green's Encyclopaedia of Medicine and Surgery*, vol. 5 .

Basmajian, J.V. 1960. *Cates' Primary Anatomy*. The Williams and Williams Company, Baltimore, 4th ed.

Bowering, Marilyn. 1989. *To All Appearances A Lady*. Harper Perennial, Toronto.

Brand, Dr. Paul, and Yancey, Philip. 1993. *Pain: The Gift Nobody Wants*. Harper Collins Publishers; Zondervan.

Brubaker, Merlin L. 1976. "Leprosy." In *Tropical Medicine*. Hunter, George W., Swartzwelder, J. Clyde, and Clyde, David F., eds. W.B. Saunders Company, Philadelphia, London, Toronto.

Ford, Laura. 1990. "Out of sight, out of mind: Sixty-five years of leper colonies in British Columbia." *The Advocate*, vol. 48.

Foster, Frank P., ed. 1897. "Chaulmoogra Oil." In *Reference Book of Practical Therapeutics*. D. Appelton & Co., vol. 1.

French, Diana. 1995a. "Historical and Archaeological Investigations of the D'Arcy Island Leper Colony, 1891-1924." *The Midden*, 28/1, Spring.

————. 1995b. *Ideology, politics and power: the socio-historical implications of the archaeology of the D'Arcy Island leper colony, 1891-1924*. PhD thesis, University of British Columbia, Vancouver, B.C.

Gelber, Robert H. 1995. "Leprosy (Hansen's Disease)." In *Principles and Practice of Infectious Diseases*, 4th ed. Mandell, Gerald L., Bennett, John E. and Dolin, Raphael, eds. Churchill Livingstone, New York, Edinburgh, London, Madrid, Melbourne, Milan, Tokyo.

Gourley, Ilma C. Salazar. 1985. "D'Arcy Island, 1891-1907." *British Columbia Historical News*, vol. 18, no. 3.

Gussow, Zachary. 1989. *Leprosy, Racism, and Public Health*. Westview Press, Boulder, San Francisco & London.

Hall, Ernest, M.D. and Nelson, John. 1898. "The Lepers of D'Arcy Island." *Dominion Medical Monthly and Ontario Medical Journal,* vol. XL, no. 6.

Hewer, Tony. 2000. *Archaeological inventory and impact assessment, D'Arcy Island Provincial Park, British Columbia.* I.R. Wilson Consultants Ltd., Victoria.

Johnson, Penelope. 1995. "BC's 'Island of Death' Marked a Sad Chapter in Canada's Medical History." *Canadian Medical Association Journal,* vol. 152, no. 6.

Lai, Chuen-yan David. 1991. *The Forbidden City Within Victoria.* Orca Book Publishers, Victoria.

Leprosy Act, 1906. Statutes of Canada, c. 24.

Losier, M.J.and Pinet, C. 1984. *Children of Lazarus: The Story of the Lazaretto at Tracadie.* Fiddlehead Poetry Books and Goose Lane Editions, Fredericton, N.B.

Manson, Patrick. 1901. "Leprosy." In *Text-Book of Medicine.* Gibson, George Alexander, ed. Young J. Pentland, Edinburgh and London.

McGinnis, Janice Dickin. 1984. "Unclean, Unclean: Canadian reaction to lepers and leprosy." In *Health, Disease and Medicine: Essays in Canadian History.* Roland, Charles G., ed. Clark Irwin (1983) Inc.

Morton, James. 1974. *In The Sea of Sterile Mountains: The Chinese in British Columbia.* J.J. Douglas Ltd., Vancouver.

Muller, J.E. 1980. *Geology of Victoria.* Geological Survey of Canada, Map 1553A.

Murphy, Patrick. 1996. "Leper Colony Largely Forgotten." Victoria *Times Colonist,* January 12.

Osler, William. 1899. "Leprosy." In *The Principles and Practice of Medicine,* 3ed.

Pojar, Jim, and MacKinnon, Andy. 1994. *Plants of Coastal British Columbia.* Lone Pine Publishing, Vancouver.

Starkin, Ed. 1976. "A B.C. Leper Colony." *Raincoast Chronicles.* No. 1. Harbour Publishing, Pender Harbour, B.C.

Teece, Philip. 1985. "Is Little D'Arcy Haunted?" *Pacific Yachting,* September.

Thomson, Richard E. 1981. *Oceanography of the British Columbia Coast.* Canada Department of Fisheries and Oceans, Special Publication 56.

Tomlinson, Alice. 1979. " Islands of the Living Dead." Victoria *Daily Colonist,* Sunday, September 2, 1979.

Wickberg, E.B. 1988. "Chinese" In *The Canadian Encyclopaedia,*vol. 1. Hurtig Publishers, Edmonton.

Wolferstan, Bill. 1976. *Cruising Guide to the Gulf Islands.* Pacific Yachting, Vancouver.

Internet

Action Program for the Elimination of Leprosy, World Health Organisation. Http://www.who.int/lep/

Infectious Diseases. Leprosy (Hansen's Disease). Encyclopaedia Britannica. Britannica Online. Http://www.eb.com

Leprosy (Hansen's Disease). Medical Information. Http://www.drugbase.co.za/data/med_info/leprosy.htm

Leprosy. Http://web.raex.com/~bbeechy/

Map of Leprosy in the World, 1998. Http://www.lepra.org.uk/where.htm

Storrs, Eleanor E. Leprosy throughout the ages.
  Http://pandoras- box.org/my05002.htm

The 15th International Congress On Leprosy—Beijing, September, 1998. Http://www.webspawner.com/users/BeijingLepCong/

The history of leprosy—(H.D.). Http://www.webspawner.com/users/LEPHISTORY/

Newspaper Articles

Victoria *Daily Colonist* 1891 to 1959

Victoria *Daily Times* 1891 to 1932

Vancouver *Province* 1901 to 1929

Vancouver *Daily News-Advertiser* 1891

Vancouver *Daily World* 1891

City of Victoria Archives

Annual Reports of Committees

Sanitary Committee Reports, 1891-1892

Medical Health Officer Reports, 1893-1905

City Council Minutes, 1891-1899

British Columbia Archives (Textual Records Searched)

Attorney General Correspondence, 1872-1937. Call No. GR-0429.

Canada Department of Agriculture. William Head Quarantine Station, 1902-1932.
  Call No. GR-2005. Microfilm No. B08648.

Central Registry of Immigration Branch. Call No. GR-1547.

General Registry of Chinese Immigration, 1885-1903. Microfilm Nos. B1020-1023.

Chinese Immigration Act, 1891-1932. Call No. C10659. Microfilm Nos. B1253-B1257.

Coroner's Inquests, 1862-1937. Call No. GR-1327.

Lieutenant Governor's Records, 1871-1936. Call No. GR-0443.
Provincial Library. Sessional Clipping Books of the Legislative Assembly. Call No.
     GR-1480. Reel Nos. B254, 255, 256.
Provincial Secretary Correspondence, Inward. 1892-1917. Call No. GR-1330.
Provincial Secretary Correspondence, Outward. 1873-1918. Call No. GR-0540.
Records of the Registrar of Shipping. Call No. GR-1237.
St. Andrew's Presbyterian Church Records, 1866-1953. Call No. MS-1507.
Surveys and Land Records. Call No. GR-1088.
Vital Statistics Agency. Death Registrations. Call No. GR-2951.

National Archives

Department of Agriculture, RG 17, File Series A1.1, AV.3.
National Health and Welfare, RG 29, Vols. 768, 769, 2577-3141.
Secretary of State, RG 6, Series A-1, Vol. 88.

British Columbia Parks, Southern Vancouver Island District.
Archaeological and Historical Site Survey Forms.
Longmore, Malcolm. 1980. D'Arcy Islands.
Park status sheets.

Photo Credits

B.C. Government, p. 58 top.
Victoria City Archives, p. 66, p. 72 top, p. 103.
British Columbia Archives and Records Service (BCARS)
     p. 72 bottom (A-01972), p. 79 (D-04782), p. 81 (D-04783), p. 104 (F-05162),
     p. 106 (F-05164), p. 109 (F-05166), p. 112 (F-05163).

Index